Improving Aural Comprehension

Improving Aural Comprehension

Joan Morley

Under the Auspices of the
English Language Institute
at the University of Michigan

STUDENT'S WORKBOOK

Ann Arbor
The University of Michigan Press

Copyright © by The University of Michigan 1972
All rights reserved
ISBN 0-472-08665-0
Library of Congress Catalog Card No. 70-185904
Published in the United States of America by
The University of Michigan Press and simultaneously
in Rexdale, Canada, by John Wiley & Sons Canada, Limited
Manufactured in the United States of America

1988   1987   1986   1985   21   20   19   18

Acknowledgments

Many colleagues and many students have contributed generously to the preparation of *Improving Aural Comprehension*. I want to thank Professor Ronald Wardhaugh for the opportunity to undertake the project and for his reading of the manuscripts. I want to express special appreciation to the many teachers who used the lessons in experimental stages and made various suggestions. A special debt of gratitude is hereby expressed to Nancy Carroll, Larry Nessly, and Lynn Jacob for their help on the initial draft and to Marvin Kierstead for final proofreading. Special words of thanks go to Kathryn Notestine for office management of all materials, to Charlotte Sebastian for her patient work on all drafts of the manuscripts, and to James Bixler, studio engineer, for his painstaking work on the recording of the entire text. Finally, particular thanks to students Behzad Khanami and Raul Elizondo who were especially generous with their time and suggestions.

Joan Morley

Introduction

The only way to improve aural comprehension is to spend many hours practicing listening. However, a directed program of purposeful listening can shorten the time. The workbook and the teacher's book of readings for *Improving Aural Comprehension* present the first part of such a program. Aural comprehension is defined as "listening with understanding" and emphasizes language skill **beyond** basic auditory discrimination and aural grammar.

This series of lessons in listening is intended for use by upper-level secondary school students and adults who are studying English as a foreign language. It is planned for use as a textbook for aural comprehension/pronunciation classes or as a supplementary text in a basic English program. It is intended for students who have had at least one course in English. Tapes are available for all lessons.

MEMORY — CONCENTRATION AND URGENCY

Many students feel that aural comprehension is hard for them. Although they can understand a sentence when they hear it, they cannot remember it a few seconds later. The difficulty experienced by many students in aural comprehension work appears to be caused by a fear of forgetting. The problem becomes more serious as the length of the material increases.

To meet this problem, a basic concern in planning this program has been to stress memory and memory span in English. Students are encouraged to repeat to themselves and in a sense "re-hear."

Psychologists who specialize in memory point out two important factors necessary for good memory—*concentration* and the degree of *urgency* for remembering. In order to include these two factors, this book emphasizes:

1. concentrated *disciplined* listening

2. immediate *writing* to provide an *urgency for remembering*.

LISTENING TASKS

This program guides the student in *what* to listen for, *when* to listen, and *how* to listen. The listening lessons in Units One through Seven focus student attention on listening, remembering, and writing facts in each of these CONCEPT areas: numbers, letters, directions, times, dates, measurements, proportions and amounts. In addition, the lessons will give practice with facts involving people, places, things, actions, events, and descriptions in the CONTENT areas of geography, history, science, mathematics, language, culture and customs, government, economics, and international affairs. Unit Eight combines all kinds of facts in a series of fifteen graded readings which provide summary practice. They give practice in understanding *who, did what, when, where* and *how.* Some lessons are as short as three or four minutes of writing time. No lesson is longer than fifteen minutes of writing time.

The main emphasis of the workbook is on factual listening. Secondary emphasis is on abstracting, analyzing, and organizing. In order to accomplish these two goals, the student is asked to do two things in each lesson:

1. write material from dictation

2. listen to and answer aural comprehension questions.

The student is asked to follow these rules for good listening:

1. DO NOT TALK.

2. CONCENTRATE YOUR ATTENTION – FORCE YOURSELF TO CONCENTRATE.

3. REPEAT THE WORDS TO YOURSELF – IN ENGLISH – TO HELP YOU REMEMBER.

GETTING THE FACTS

Finally, improving aural comprehension demands many hours of practice. A program of directed listening can shorten the time. It is the purpose of this workbook to provide carefully planned and graded listening lessons to help students learn to *listen and get facts* – so they are ready to *listen and get ideas.* The next part of a total listening program would emphasize listening and understanding *both* facts and abstract relationships.

Contents

Unit 1

Numbers and
Numerical Relationships

Unit 1

Numbers and
Numerical Relationships

Numbers probably are used more every day than any other kind of factual information. Immediate recognition and understanding are necessary for good aural comprehension. This unit is a short course in basic number concepts and uses as they are expressed in English. Be sure to ask questions and discuss the unit with your teacher. The goals of this unit are:

... to give practice with numbers

... to present numerical vocabulary words and phrases

... to provide practice with typical statistical information.

All the lessons are relatively short. Some are as short as three or four minutes of writing time. The first part of the unit provides six *Review Lessons*. It is important to do each of these carefully. Some of them may seem very easy, but they include important review work in auditory discrimination and reading and writing hundreds, thousands, and millions rapidly. The second part of the unit presents seven *Context Lessons* including short aural arithmetic practice, writing personal data (telephone numbers and addresses) and practice with statistics. The third part of the unit includes five *Problem Lessons*. They provide realistic use of numbers as you will find them in your studies: page numbers, library classification numbers, and comparative statistics. The two *Test Lessons* present practical word problems.

NUMERAL SYSTEM

The numeral system we use is called the Arabic system. Arabic numerals are 1, 2, 3, 4, etc. The numbers used to count the objects in a group are called *cardinal* numbers: 1, 2, 3, etc. Those used to indicate position or order in a list are called *ordinal* numbers: 1st, 2nd, 3rd, 4th, etc. The *odd* numbers are those beginning with 1 and counting by twos: 1, 3, 5, 7, 9, etc. The *even* numbers are those beginning with 2 and counting by twos: 2, 4, 6, 8, 10, etc.

Listen carefully as the following dictation is read. Have your pencil ready to write. Listen to the sentence. Remember the number. Write the number in the blank. Write the numbers in figures not words. Follow the examples.

Cardinal Numbers

Example: She is __16__ years old.

1. The coat cost _____ dollars.

2. John bought _____ new ties.

3. Bill wears size _____ .

4. The temperature is _____ .

5. The bus arrived at _____ o'clock.

6. Leap year has _____ days.

7. Sue is _____ years old.

8. Jan was _____ minutes late.

9. Tony got _____ on the last test.

10. There are _____ sentences in this list.

Ordinal Numbers

Example: It is the __25 TH__ of May.

1. California is the _____ largest state.

2. Alaska was the _____ state.

3. Bob's birthday is on the _____ of May.

4. The theater is on _____ Street.

5. This is the _____ Century.

6. Our seats are in the _____ row.

7. Henry _____ was a good king.

8. This is the _____ Congress.

9. Jim was _____ in his class.

10. This is the _____ sentence in this list.

Check your answers. Then turn the page and wait for the aural comprehension questions.*

_____

*When you finish this lesson turn to page 5 and study the spelling and pronunciation list. Turn to page 6 and practice writing the numbers.

AURAL COMPREHENSION QUESTIONS

Listen and remember the first question. Turn back to the previous page and find the answer. Write the answer here. Do the same for each of the other questions. Write short answers only.

Answer to Question 1. _____

Answer to Question 2. _____

Answer to Question 3. _____

Answer to Question 4. _____

DISCUSSION TOPICS

1. Ordinal and cardinal uses.

2. Odd number and even number uses.

3. Uses of suffix endings *-st, -nd, -rd,* and *-th.*

VOCABULARY AND PRONUNCIATION

Practice each phrase or word aloud. Listen to the teacher's pronunciation. Imitate sounds, syllable accents, and intonation patterns. Be sure you know the meaning of each word.

numbers	odd numbers	cardinal numbers
numeral system	even numbers	count objects
Arabic numbers	counting by two's	ordinal numbers
Arabic numerals	every other number	tell position
figures	suffixes	tell order
	fir*st*	
	seco*nd*	
	thi*rd*	
	four*th*	

NUMBERS — CORRECT SPELLING

Use this page as a spelling and pronunciation reference sheet.

one	1	first	1st	eleven	11	eleventh	11th
two	2	second	2nd	twelve	12	twelfth	12th
three	3	third	3rd	thirteen	13	thirteenth	13th
four	4	fourth	4th	fourteen	14	fourteenth	14th
five	5	fifth	5th	fifteen	15	fifteenth	15th
six	6	sixth	6th	sixteen	16	sixteenth	16th
seven	7	seventh	7th	seventeen	17	seventeenth	17th
eight	8	eighth	8th	eighteen	18	eighteenth	18th
nine	9	ninth	9th	nineteen	19	nineteenth	19th
ten	10	tenth	10th	twenty	20	twentieth	20th

twenty-one	21	twenty-first	21st
twenty-two	22	twenty-second	22nd
twenty-three	23	twenty-third	23rd
twenty-four	24	twenty-fourth	24th
twenty-five	25	twenty-fifth	25th
twenty-six	26	twenty-sixth	26th
twenty-seven	27	twenty-seventh	27th
twenty-eight	28	twenty-eighth	28th
twenty-nine	29	twenty-ninth	29th
thirty	30	thirtieth	30th
forty	40	fortieth	40th
fifty	50	fiftieth	50th
sixty	60	sixtieth	60th
seventy	70	seventieth	70th
eighty	80	eightieth	80th
ninety	90	ninetieth	90th
one hundred	100	one hundredth	100th
one thousand	1000	one thousandth	1000th

NUMBERS – WRITTEN FORMS

Practice writing these figures.

1   2   3   4   5

6   7   8   9   10

1st   2nd   3rd   4th   5th

6th   7th   8th   9th   10th

DISCRIMINATING BETWEEN TEENS AND TENS

"Did he say thirty or thirteen? Did she say seventeen or seventy?"

The teen numbers, those between thirteen and nineteen, are often confused with the multiples of ten: thirty, forty, fifty, sixty, seventy, eighty, and ninety. This lesson is for practice in hearing the differences in the following pairs of numbers: 13-30, 14-40, 15-50, 16-60, 17-70, 18-80, 19-90. It is important to listen to the last part of each word.

Listen carefully. Be ready to write. Draw a circle around the correct number.

1. The student from Norway bought (40 − 14) books.

2. The student from Turkey paid (30 − 13) dollars for a book.

3. One of the Thai students lost (18 − 80) dollars the first day of class.

4. He asked the man at the post office for (30 − 13) eight-cent stamps.

5. It costs (50 − 15) cents to call Chicago.

6. He lives at (1762 − 7062) North Connecticut Avenue.

7. He bought (90 − 19) new pencils.

8. Her address is (3041 − 1341) Island Drive.

9. He paid (80 − 18) cents for a hundred sheets of paper.

10. Cheap typing paper costs only (19 − 90) cents for a hundred sheets.

11. The bus was (16 − 60) minutes late leaving for the airport.

12. It took (15 − 50) hours to finish the work.

13. The student from Mexico lives at (1662 − 6062) LaSalle Street.

14. He finished the test in (17 − 70) minutes.

Check your answers. Then turn the page and wait for the aural comprehension questions.

AURAL COMPREHENSION QUESTIONS

Listen and remember the first question. Turn back to the previous page and find the answer. Write the answer here. Do the same for each of the other questions. Always write short answers only.

1. _____

2. _____

3. _____

4. _____

5. _____

DISCUSSION TOPICS

1. Difficult pairs of numbers.

2. Syllable accent for teen numbers.

3. Syllable accent for multiples of ten.

VOCABULARY AND PRONUNCIATION

Practice aloud. Imitate the teacher's pronunciation of the words and phrases — sounds, syllable accents, and intonation. Discuss meanings.

teen numbers	thirteen — thirty
multiples of ten	fourteen — forty
hear the difference	fifteen — fifty
discriminate	sixteen — sixty
	seventeen — seventy
	eighteen — eighty
	nineteen — ninety

PRACTICE WITH ORDINALS

"Did he say first or third? Did he say 25th or 26th?"

Some of the ordinal numbers are hard to understand in rapid speech. Certain ones are confused easily with others. This lesson is for practice with confusing pairs of ordinals. Listen to the suffix ending of each number.

Listen carefully. Draw a circle around the correct number.

1. The Olympic games began in the (4th — 5th) Century B.C.

2. The (3rd — 1st) Roman governor built a huge stadium.

3. Baseball fans celebrated the (18th — 80th) anniversary of baseball last year.

4. The game will be on the (22nd — 27th) of April.

5. The (1st — 4th) Monte Carlo Rally was held in 1924.

6. This year is the (25th — 29th) year of professional hockey.

7. Eddie Arcaro, a famous jockey, rode his (246th — 245th) horse last year.

8. Last year was the (118th — 180th) year of the horse race called the Kentucky Derby.

9. The football season begins on the (23rd — 21st) of September.

10. The baseball season begins on the (22nd — 27th) of April.

11. The hockey season begins on the (25th — 29th) of November.

12. The team from Mexico won (1st — 4th) place in the tennis match.

13. Last year the (4th — 5th) winter Olympics were held in Sweden.

14. This is the (6th — 5th) year in which soccer championship playoffs have been held.

AURAL COMPREHENSION QUESTIONS

Listen to each question carefully. Write the answer.

1. _____

2. _____

3. _____

4. _____

DISCUSSION TOPICS

1. Uses of ordinal numbers.

2. Sports in your country.

VOCABULARY AND PRONUNCIATION

Practice aloud. Discuss meanings.

fourth	– fifth	Olympic games	jockey
first	– third	winter Olympics	professional hockey
fourth	– first	Roman governor	football season
fifth	– ninth	stadium	baseball season
fifth	– sixth	celebrated	hockey season
second	– seventh	anniversary	team
eightieth	– eighteenth	baseball	won 6th place
		Monte Carlo Rally	soccer
		Kentucky Derby	championship
		horse race	playoffs

HUNDREDS: READING AND WRITING NUMBERS TO A THOUSAND

"What are the hundreds?"

The hundreds are any of the 3-digit numbers from 100 to 999. The hundreds consist of three digits. The first digit on the right is called the *ones* digit. The next is called the *tens* digit. The third is the *hundreds* digit.

```
    7         2         5
    |         |         |
    ↓         ↓         ↓
  seven
  hundred   twenty - five
```

Thus, seven, two, five, is read seven hundred twenty-five.* This lesson will give practice in writing hundreds rapidly from dictation.

Listen carefully. Write the numbers as they are read.

Column 1	Column 2	Column 3	Column 4
_____	_____	_____	_____
_____	_____	_____	_____
_____	_____	_____	_____
_____	_____	_____	_____

Column 5	Column 6	Column 7	Column 8
_____	_____	_____	_____
_____	_____	_____	_____
_____	_____	_____	_____
_____	_____	_____	_____

———

*Or, seven hundred *and* twenty-five.

11

AURAL COMPREHENSION QUESTIONS

Listen to each question carefully.

1. _____   3. _____

2. _____   4. _____

DISCUSSION TOPICS

1. Definitions of figure and digit.

2. Reading hundreds with a zero place-holder (i.e., 105, 609, 402, 304, 707, etc.)

VOCABULARY AND PRONUNCIATION

Practice aloud. Discuss meanings.

hundreds

from 100 to 999

from a hundred to nine hundred and ninety-nine

_____

the ones digit (or place)

the tens digit (or place)

the hundreds digit (or place)

on the right

_____

two hundred forty-three   (243)

one hundred eight   (108) ⎫
                          ⎬ (three
one hundred and eight   (108) ⎪ alternate
                          ⎪ ways to
a hundred and eight   (108) ⎭ read 108)

place-holder zero   (504)

a number

a figure*

a digit†

3-digit number

_____

add

addition (5 + 5 = 10)

total

problem (i.e., addition problem)

_____

smallest number

lowest number (i.e., lowest value)

largest number

highest number (i.e., highest value)

---

* A figure is a printed or written number symbol — not a word.

† A digit is any single Arabic numeral from 0 to 9.

THOUSANDS: READING AND WRITING NUMBERS TO A MILLION

"What are the thousands?"

The thousands are any of the 4-digit, 5-digit, or 6-digit numbers from 1000 to 999,999. The thousands are written 1,000, 2,000, 3,000, etc. The ten-thousands are written 10,000; 20,000; 30,000, etc. The hundred-thousands are written 100,000; 200,000; 300,000, etc. For easy reading, numbers of more than four digits are separated by commas into groups of three digits each, beginning at the right.

7	8	2,	6	4	1
↓	↓	↓	↓	↓	↓
seven hundred	eighty -	two thousand,	six hundred	forty -	one

This number is read seven hundred eighty-two thousand, six hundred forty-one. This lesson will give practice in writing thousands rapidly from dictation.

Listen carefully. Write the numbers as they are read. Work as rapidly as you can.

Column 1 _____   *Column 2* _____

_____   _____

_____   _____

_____   _____

_____   _____

Column 3 _____

_____

_____

_____

_____

_____

AURAL COMPREHENSION QUESTIONS

Listen to each question carefully. Write a key word to help you.

1. _____   3. _____

_____   _____

_____   _____

2. _____   4. _____

_____   _____

_____   _____

DISCUSSION TOPICS

1. Reading and writing thousands; using *commas,* not periods.*

2. Ways to state subtraction and multiplication problems.

VOCABULARY AND PRONUNCIATION

Practice aloud. Discuss meanings.

4-digit number	subtract from (i.e., take-away from)
5-digit number	subtraction $(5 - 1 = 4)$
6-digit number	difference
thousands	multiply by
ten-thousands	multiplication $(10 \times 2 = 20)$
hundred-thousands	10 times 6

seven thousand six hundred and forty-two (7,642)	comma
ten thousand seventy-five (10,075)	separated by commas
fifteen thousand six (15,006)	groups of 3 digits
a hundred and one thousand and one (101,001)	beginning at the right

———

*In English a period used with numbers indicates a decimal point.

MILLIONS: READING AND WRITING NUMBERS TO A BILLION

"What are the millions?"

The millions are any of the 7-digit, 8-digit, or 9-digit numbers from 1,000,000 to 999,999,999. Ten millions are written like this — 40,000,000. Hundred-millions are written like this — 500,000,000. (A thousand million is called one billion.)

5	4	6 ,	0	8	5 ,	6	0	9
↓	↓	↓		↓	↓	↓		↓
five hundred	forty -	six million		eighty -	five thousand	six hundred		nine

This number is read 546 million*, 85 thousand*, 6 hundred* and 9. This lesson will give practice in writing millions from dictation.

Listen carefully. Write the numbers as they are read. Work as rapidly as you can.

1. _____

2. _____

3. _____

4. _____

*Notice the *singular* forms of million, thousand, and hundred.

15

AURAL COMPREHENSION QUESTIONS

Listen to each question carefully.

1. _____   3. _____

   _____   _____

   _____   _____

2. _____   4. _____

   _____   _____

   _____   _____

DISCUSSION TOPICS

1. Reading millions.

2. Different ways to write division problems.

$$5\overline{)25}^{\,5}$$

VOCABULARY AND PRONUNCIATION

Practice aloud. Discuss meanings.

millions   divide

ten-millions   division

hundred-millions   divide 5 into 10

                              divide 25 by 5

MULTIPLICATION AND DIVISION

"What is 4 times 4? What is 2 into 38?"

The table given below is a "short-cut" aid to multiplication and division problems. It is called the Pythagoras Table. This is the way to use it:

Multiplication

What is 13 times 8?

To find the answer:

   (1)   Find 13 on the top

   (2)   Find 8 on the left

   (3)   Find the square where they meet

Division

What is 8 into 104?

To find the answer:

   (1)   Find 8 on the left

   (2)   Find 104 in that same line.

   (3)   Find the number at the top of that column

Listen to the problems as they are read. Find the answers as quickly as possible. Write them below.

1	2	3	4	5	6	7	8	9	10	11	12	13	14	15	16	17	18	19	20
2	4	6	8	10	12	14	16	18	20	22	24	26	28	30	32	34	36	38	40
3	6	9	12	15	18	21	24	27	30	33	36	39	42	45	48	51	54	57	60
4	8	12	16	20	24	28	32	36	40	44	48	52	56	60	64	68	72	76	80
5	10	15	20	25	30	35	40	45	50	55	60	65	70	75	80	85	90	95	100
6	12	18	24	30	36	42	48	54	60	66	72	78	84	90	96	102	108	114	120
7	14	21	28	35	42	49	56	63	70	77	84	91	98	105	112	119	126	133	140
8	16	24	32	40	48	56	64	72	80	88	96	104	112	120	128	136	144	152	160
9	18	27	36	45	54	63	72	81	90	99	108	117	126	135	144	153	162	171	180
10	20	30	40	50	60	70	80	90	100	110	120	130	140	150	160	170	180	190	200

Multiplication:

(1) _____ (5) _____

(2) _____ (6) _____

(3) _____ (7) _____

(4) _____ (8) _____

Division:

(1) _____ (5) _____

(2) _____ (6) _____

(3) _____ (7) _____

(4) _____ (8) _____

AURAL COMPREHENSION QUESTIONS

Listen to each question carefully.

The number 3 is the square root of 9; 4 is the square root of 16.

1. _____

2. _____

3. _____

4. _____

DISCUSSION TOPIC

1. Square root.*

VOCABULARY AND PRONUNCIATION

Practice aloud. Discuss meanings.

table of numbers

short-cut

square root

6 is the square root of 36

---

*Square root is a factor of a number which when squared gives you the number. Three is the square root of nine.

AURAL ARITHMETIC

"How many? How much?"

It is important to be able to do rapid aural arithmetic. See how fast you can work.

Listen carefully. Write the problems as they are read.

Follow these examples:

$$
\begin{array}{r}
104 \\
148 \\
+\quad 11 \\
\hline
\end{array}
\qquad
\begin{array}{r}
231 \\
-\quad 10 \\
\hline
\end{array}
\qquad
\begin{array}{r}
24 \\
\times\quad 2 \\
\hline
\end{array}
\qquad
2\,\overline{)\,34}
$$

Addition	Subtraction	Multiplication	Division
1.)	1.)	1.)	1.)
2.)	2.)	2.)	2.)
3.)	3.)	3.)	3.)
4.)	4.)	4.)	4.)

AURAL COMPREHENSION QUESTIONS

Listen to each question carefully.

1. _____   3. _____

2. _____   4. _____

DISCUSSION TOPIC

1. Alternate ways of stating arithmetic problems.

VOCABULARY AND PRONUNCIATION

Practice aloud. Discuss meanings.

subtraction

$$\begin{array}{r} 10 \quad \text{minuend} \\ -\ 1 \quad \text{subtrahend} \\ \hline 9 \quad \text{difference} \end{array}$$

$$(10 - 1 = 9)$$
minus

20 minus 4 is 16

10 take away 2 is 8

subtract 5 from 10

take 5 away from 10

addition

$$\begin{array}{r} 6 \quad \text{addend} \\ +\ 4 \quad \text{addend} \\ \hline 10 \quad \text{sum} \end{array}$$

$$(6 + 4 = 10)$$
plus

3 plus 3 is 6

6 and 6 are 12

add 3 and 2

multiplication

$$\begin{array}{r} 42 \quad \text{multiplicand} \\ \times\ 2 \quad \text{multiplier} \\ \hline 84 \quad \text{product} \end{array}$$

$$(42 \times 2 = 84)$$
times

6 times 2 is 12

division

divisor 5 $\overline{)25}$ dividend, 5 quotient

$$(25 \div 5 = 5)$$
divided by

2 into 10   2 $\overline{)10}$

5 goes into 25   5 $\overline{)25}$

10 divided by 2   2 $\overline{)10}$

TELEPHONE NUMBERS

"What is your telephone number? What number did you want?"

Getting telephone numbers written down correctly is important both for business and social reasons. Local telephone numbers in the United States have seven digits. The name of each digit is usually pronounced individually. For example, this number (764-2417) is pronounced, "seven, six, four . . . two, four, one, seven."

To make long distance calls you must put three area code digits *before* the local number.

Listen carefully. Write the telephone number with a dash after the first three numbers (664-2417). Then write the area code numbers.

Local Number	*Area Code*
1. _____	(_____) Miami, Florida
2. _____	(_____) Cleveland, Ohio
3. _____	(_____) Detroit, Michigan
4. _____	(_____) New Orleans, Louisiana
5. _____	(_____) Boston, Massachusetts
6. _____	(_____) Washington, D.C.
7. _____	(_____) New York City, New York
8. _____	(_____) Tucson, Arizona
9. _____	(_____) Philadelphia, Pennsylvania
10. _____	(_____) Seattle, Washington

AURAL COMPREHENSION QUESTIONS

Listen to each question carefully.

1. _____

2. _____

3. _____

4. _____

DISCUSSION TOPICS

1. Area codes.

2. Long distance direct dialing; collect calls — reverse the charges.

3. Using the telephone book.

4. Person-to-person; station-to-station.

VOCABULARY AND PRONUNCIATION

Practice aloud. Discuss meanings.

telephone number	social	long distance calls
business	local numbers	area code

Miami	Florida
Cleveland	Ohio
Detroit	Michigan
New Orleans	Louisiana
Boston	Massachusetts
New York City	New York (state)
Tucson	Arizona
Philadelphia	Pennsylvania
Seattle	Washington (state)
Washington, D.C.	

ADDRESSES

"What's your address? Where do you live? What's your house number?"

In the United States the number is given first and is followed by the name of the street, avenue, boulevard, or drive. These two items are written on the same line. Next the names of the city and the state are written and are followed by the zip code number. The zip code may be written below.

Listen carefully. Write the addresses following this example:

1324 Main Street
Ann Arbor, Michigan 48105

1. _____ Market St.

   San Francisco, Calif. _____

2. _____ Mission St.

   San Francisco, Calif. _____

3. _____ _____

   _____ _____

4. _____ Michigan Ave.

   Chicago, Ill. _____

5. _____ Congress St.

   _____ _____

6. _____ _____

   _____ _____

7. _____ Woodward Ave.

   Detroit, Mich. _____

8. _____ Grand River Ave.

   _____ _____

9. _____ _____

   _____ _____

10. _____ Hanover St.

    Baltimore, Md. _____

11. _____ Fremont St.

    _____ _____

12. _____ _____

    _____ _____

SUGGESTION: After this lesson you may wish to begin work on Unit Two (page 47) and alternate lessons from Units One and Two.

AURAL COMPREHENSION QUESTIONS

Listen to each question carefully.

1. _____

2. _____

3. _____

4. _____

DISCUSSION TOPICS

1.   Zip code (book at Post Office).

2.   Forwarding addresses.

VOCABULARY AND PRONUNCIATION

Practice aloud. Discuss meanings.

address	Market Street (St.)	San Francisco
house number	Mission Street	California (Calif.)
street address	Michigan Avenue (Ave.)	Chicago
avenue	Congress Street	Illinois (Ill.)
boulevard	Woodward Avenue	Detroit
drive	Grand River Avenue	Michigan (Mich.)
zip code	Hanover Street	Baltimore
He lives at _____ .	Fremont Street	Maryland (Md.)
His address is _____ .		

STATISTICAL DATA
WORLD METROPOLITAN AREAS — POPULATION

"What is the population of Tokyo? How big is London?"

A metropolitan area is defined as a large city plus neighboring cities which are connected by continuous building. In addition more distant cities are included if most of their population is supported by commuters to the central city. These figures are based on United Nations estimates.

Listen carefully. Write the population figures. Remember to use commas correctly as: 7,200,000.

Metropolitan Area   *Population*

1. Tokyo-Yokohama (Japan) _____

2. New York City (U.S.A.) _____

3. Osaka-Kobe-Kyoto (Japan) _____

4. London (United Kingdom) _____

5. Moscow (Soviet Union) _____

6. Buenos Aires (Argentina) _____

7. Paris (France) _____

8. Los Angeles (U.S.A.) _____

9. Calcutta (India) _____

10. Shanghai (Mainland China) _____

11. Chicago (U.S.A.) _____

12. Mexico City (Mexico) _____

13. São Paulo (Brazil) _____

14. Rio de Janeiro (Brazil) _____

15. Bombay (India) _____

16. Cairo (Egypt) _____

17. Essen-Dortmund-Duisburg (The Ruhr-West Germany) _____

18. Philadelphia-Trenton-Wilmington (U.S.A.) _____

19. Peking (Mainland China) _____

20. Detroit (U.S.A.) - Windsor (Canada) _____

AURAL COMPREHENSION QUESTIONS

Listen to each question carefully.

1. _____   3. _____

_____   4. _____

_____

2. _____

_____

_____

DISCUSSION TOPICS

1. Round figures; rounding off;* just over; just under.

2. Accuracy of these statistics today.

3. Consult an almanac and compare current population statistics with these.

VOCABULARY AND PRONUNCIATION

Practice aloud. Discuss meanings.

metropolitan area	based on	Japan	Mainland China
population	estimates	U.S.A.	Mexico
central city	approximate	United Kingdom	Brazil
neighboring cities	round figures	Soviet Union (U.S.S.R.)	Egypt
continuous building	round off to the nearest million	Argentina	The Ruhr
more distant cities	just over	France	West Germany
supported by commuters	just under	India	Canada

_____

*Round figures are approximate figures in which fractions are adjusted in one of two ways: (1) if half or over, move to the next highest number or (2) if under half, move to the next lowest.

STATISTICAL DATA
LANGUAGES OF THE WORLD

"How many people speak Spanish? How many speak French?"

Over 150 languages of the world have at least one million speakers. The following twenty-two languages have been selected for comparative study. The statistics are United Nations estimates.

Listen carefully. Write the statistical information as rapidly as possible. Remember to use commas correctly as: 106,592,000.

1. Arabic _____

2. Burmese _____

3. Chinese (Cantonese) _____

4. Chinese (Mandarin) _____

5. English _____

6. French _____

7. German _____

8. Greek _____

9. Hindi _____

10. Italian _____

11. Japanese _____

12. Korean _____

13. Persian _____

14. Polish _____

15. Portuguese _____

16. Russian _____

17. Spanish _____

18. Swedish _____

19. Thai _____

20. Turkish _____

21. Urdu _____

22. Vietnamese _____

AURAL COMPREHENSION QUESTIONS

Listen to each question carefully.

1. _____

2. _____

3. _____

4. _____

DISCUSSION TOPICS

1. Range; rank order.*

2. Languages; contrast the narrow and the widespread geographical locations.

3. Accuracy of these statistics today. (Consult an almanac and compare current statistics with these.)

4. Notice the use of *the* as in this example:
    > Arabic is spoken by 101 million people.
    > The Arabic language is spoken by 101 million people.

VOCABULARY AND PRONUNCIATION

Practice aloud. Discuss meanings.

languages

comparative

statistics

statistical

(all the names of the languages on the previous page)

estimates

rank order (i.e., listed from highest to lowest)

the range

extremes of a series

---

*Rank order is numbers listed from the highest in value to the lowest in value. The range is the extremes (the numbers at each end) of such a series.

STATISTICAL DATA
POPULAR MAGAZINES

"What is the most popular magazine in the United States?"
"How many copies are sold each issue?"

The Magazine Advertising Bureau of Magazine Publishers Association provided the following recent statistics on magazine circulation per issue.

Listen to the name of the magazine. Write the figure as in the example. Example: *The Blue Magazine* 14,345,672

1. *Reader's Digest* _____

2. *TV Guide* _____

3. *McCall's* _____

4. *Family Circle* _____

5. *Life* _____

6. *Better Homes & Gardens* _____

7. *Woman's Day* _____

8. *Ladies' Home Journal* _____

9. *Good Housekeeping* _____

10. *National Geographic* _____

11. *Playboy* _____

12. *Redbook* _____

13. *Time* _____

14. *American Home* _____

15. *Farm Journal* _____

16. *American Legion* _____

17. *Boys' Life* _____

AURAL COMPREHENSION QUESTIONS

Listen to each question carefully.

1. _____

2. _____

3. _____

DISCUSSION TOPICS

1. Ratio.*

2. Favorite magazines; types of magazines.

3. Contents and readers of each magazine.

VOCABULARY AND PRONUNCIATION

Practice aloud. Discuss meanings.

highest	six to one
second highest	magazine
third highest	circulation
lowest	issue
ratio	subscription

(all the names of the magazines on the previous page)

---

*Ratio is an expression of the relationship in size, quantity, or amount between two or more things. The ratio between 100 and 50 is a ratio of 2 to 1. The ratio between 99 and 33 is 3 to 1. Be sure to write a ratio in the correct order.

PAGE NUMBERS

"What page is it on? What page did you say? What pages should we read?"

Every student knows how important it is to hear the correct page numbers. Get into the habit of getting the number the *first* time the teacher says it. Write it down immediately. If you do this you will not have to worry, you will not have to ask a friend, and you will not have to ask the teacher to repeat.

Listen carefully. Write down the page numbers as they are read. They will be given in rapid natural speech.

Page Number   *Word*

_____   _____

_____   _____

_____   _____

_____   _____

_____   _____

_____   _____

_____   _____

_____   _____

_____   _____

_____   _____

PROBLEM

Use this book. Turn to the first *Page Number* you have written on page 31. Find the first word in the title of the lesson. Write that word in the *Word* column on page 31 beside the correct page number. Do the same thing for each page number you have written. Work as rapidly as you can.

DISCUSSION TOPIC

1. Meanings of the words you have written (all the words you have written on page 31).

VOCABULARY AND PRONUNCIATION

Practice aloud. Discuss meanings.

page numbers

get into the habit

the first time

immediately

READING ASSIGNMENTS: MULTIPLE PAGE NUMBERS

"How many pages? Which pages?"

Assignments for class work are often given as follows: "Please read pages 179 through 191 and pages 205 to 211."
You must be sure to get *both* numbers written down correctly. Sometimes the prepositions *to* and *through* are used
interchangeably for multiple page numbers.

Listen carefully. Write the page numbers. You may abbreviate pages as follows: "pp. 24-25."

	Page Numbers		*How many pages?*
1. PSYCHOLOGY	_____		_____
	_____		_____
	_____		_____
	_____	Sub-total	_____
2. BIOLOGY	_____		_____
	_____		_____
	_____		_____
	_____	Sub-total	_____
3. LITERATURE	_____		_____
	_____		_____
	_____		_____
	_____	Sub-total	_____
		TOTAL	_____

PROBLEM

Add the pages for each individual assignment in Psychology. Write each total on the correct line under *How many pages.* Be sure you get the correct total for each. Subtract the smaller number from the larger number and then add 1 (to include both the beginning and ending pages.) Do the same for Biology and Literature. Then add the Psychology assignments for a sub-total in Psychology. Do the same for Biology and Literature. Then add the *sub-totals* for a *grand total.* Work as quickly as you can.

DISCUSSION TOPICS

1. Contrast this lesson's interchangeable use of prepositions "to" and "through" (to mean *all* of the *pages* between the two numbers given) with the definite meaning *difference* in reference to *chapters.* *

2. Total; sub-total; grand total.

VOCABULARY AND PRONUNCIATION

Practice aloud. Discuss meanings.

assignments   Psychology

pages   64 through 69   Biology

pages   145 to 155   Literature

sub-total   freshman

grand total   university

semester   instructor

                                                 professor

---

*"Read chapters one through four." = definitely includes number four. "Read chapters one to four" = might be interpreted as one, two, and three *or* as one, two, three, and four.

LIBRARY CLASSIFICATIONS: DEWEY DECIMAL SYSTEM

One of the major library classification systems is the Dewey Decimal System invented by Melvil Dewey. It contains ten major classifications into which all knowledge can be classified. They are listed on the next page.*

Listen carefully. Write the call numbers.

Call Number

Classification

_____

1. *Russian Grammar* _____

_____

2. *Better Photography* _____

_____

3. *Shakespeare's Plays* _____

_____

4. *Crime in the Streets* _____

_____

5. *Hinduism* _____

_____

6. *Greek Philosophy* _____

_____

7. *Human Genes* _____

_____

8. *Paintings of El Greco* _____

_____

9. *Roman Architecture* _____

_____

10. *Fall of the Roman Empire* _____

_____

*The other major library classification system is the Library of Congress system.

PROBLEM

Fill in the name of each classification on page 35. Use this reference list.

Reference

DEWEY DECIMAL SYSTEM

000-099	GENERAL WORKS	(including encyclopedias, newspapers, periodicals, bibliographies, etc.)
100-199	PHILOSOPHY	(including books on psychology, ethics, etc.)
200-299	RELIGION	(including books on Christian and non-Christian beliefs and books on classical mythology)
300-399	SOCIOLOGY	(including government, economics, education, banking, commerce, folklore, etc.)
400-499	LANGUAGE	(including grammars, dictionaries, readers, etc., in all languages)
500-599	SCIENCE	(including mathematics, astronomy, physics, geology, chemistry, biology, botany, zoology, etc.)
600-699	USEFUL ARTS	(including medicine, engineering, business, accounting, salesmanship, agriculture, etc.)
700-799	FINE ARTS	(including architecture, painting, music, amusements, etc.)
800-899	LITERATURE	(including poetry, drama, debates, essays, etc., in all languages)
900-999	TRAVEL-BIOGRAPHY-HISTORY	(travel includes all countries — biography includes persons in alphabetical order — history includes all countries and all ages)

DISCUSSION TOPICS* — VOCABULARY AND PRONUNCIATION

1. Discuss each of the Dewey Decimal classification areas.

2. Practice all new vocabulary words.

3. Library of Congress classification system.

---

*For homework consult the card catalog in the local library and bring back several call numbers for comparison.

UNIVERSITY AND COLLEGE DEGREES BY FIELDS OF SPECIALIZATION
(Part I)

The U.S. Office of Education recently released statistics on the degrees given by institutions of higher education. Let us look at some of the interesting trends and make some comparisons. These data are for the United States and possessions. It is particularly interesting to notice the fields which are dominated by men and those which are dominated by women. (See next lesson for Part 2.)

Listen carefully. Write as the teacher dictates.

	Bachelor/1st Professional Degrees	
	Men	*Women*
Agriculture		
Architecture		
Biological Sciences		
Business and Commerce		
Education		
Engineering		
English and Journalism		
Fine and Applied Arts		
Foreign Languages and Literature		
Forestry		
Geography		
Health Professions (total)*		
Dentistry (D.D.S. or D.M.D.)		
Medicine (M.D.)		
Nursing and/or Public Health		
Pharmacy		

*Includes other areas not listed here.

PROBLEM

1. List the three highest and the three lowest fields for men.

_____   _____

_____   _____

_____   _____

2. List the three highest and the three lowest fields for women.

_____   _____

_____   _____

_____   _____

DISCUSSION TOPICS

1. Answers to the problem.

2. Reasons for the numbers/lack of numbers in the above fields.

VOCABULARY AND PRONUNCIATION

Practice aloud. Discuss meanings.

university	B.A. (Bachelor of Arts)	Applied Arts
college	B.S. (Bachelor of Science)	Foreign Languages
degrees	M.D. (Medical Doctor)	Literature
fields of specialization	D.D.S. (Doctor of Dental Surgery)	Forestry
first professional degree	working on a B.A.	Geography
		Health Professions
U.S. Office of Education	Agriculture	Dentistry
statistics	Architecture	Medicine
comparisons	Biological Sciences	Nursing
outlying areas	Business and Commerce	Public Health Nursing
institution of higher education	Education	Pharmacy
trends	Engineering	
dominate	English and Journalism	
	Fine Arts	

COLLEGE DEGREES (Part 2)

The following statistics are the second part of the U.S. Office of Education information on degrees granted by institutions of higher education. Let us look at these facts and make some comparisons. (See previous lesson for Part 1.)

Listen carefully. Write as the teacher dictates.

| | Bachelor/1st Professional Degrees | |
	Men	*Women*
Home Economics		
Law		
Library Science		
Mathematical Subjects		
Philosophy		
Physical Sciences (total)*		
Chemistry		
Physics		
Psychology		
Religion		
Social Sciences (total)		
Economics		
History		
Political Science/Government		
Sociology		
Trade and Industrial Training		
TOTAL (Parts 1 and 2)*		

———

*Includes areas not listed here.

PROBLEM

Use both data sheets — the ones from Lesson 17 and Lesson 18.

1. First, list the top 5 fields for each sex in rank order. Include the statistics.

Men _____   Women _____

_____   _____

_____   _____

_____   _____

_____   _____

Total _____   Total _____

2. Then, total the enrollment for each sex in these 5 top fields.

3. Compare these figures with the totals which you just wrote on page 39.

DISCUSSION TOPIC

1. Answers to the problem.

VOCABULARY AND PRONUNCIATION

Practice aloud. Discuss meanings.

finish a degree	Home Economics	Chemistry	History
earn a degree	Law	Physics	Political Science
grant a degree	Library Science	Psychology	Government
confer a degree	Mathematical Subjects	Religion	Sociology
dominate	Philosophy	Social Sciences	Trade and Industrial Training
breakdown (noun)	Physical Sciences	Economics	

PRACTICAL PROBLEM-SOLVING (1)

Listen carefully. Write the numbers given in each problem.

1. _____

4. _____

2. _____

5. _____

3. _____

6. _____

turn the page for # 7

7. _____

_____

_____

_____

_____

9. _____

_____

_____

_____

_____

8. _____

_____

_____

_____

_____

10. _____

_____

_____

_____

_____

TEST

Do the problems. Check your answers with your teacher.

PRACTICAL PROBLEM-SOLVING (2)

Listen carefully. Write the numbers given in each problem.

1. _____

   _____

   _____

   _____

   _____

2. _____

   _____

   _____

   _____

   _____

3. _____

   _____

   _____

   _____

4. _____

   _____

   _____

   _____

   _____

5. _____

   _____

   _____

   _____

   _____

6. _____

   _____

   _____

   _____

turn the page for #7

7. _____

_____

_____

_____

_____

9. _____

_____

_____

_____

_____

8. _____

_____

_____

_____

10. _____

_____

_____

_____

TEST

Do the problems. Check your answers with your teacher.

VOCABULARY — NUMBERS AND NUMERICAL RELATIONSHIPS

Write your personal list of new words. Review this list and be sure you understand each item.

_____ _____

_____ _____

_____ _____

_____ _____

_____ _____

_____ _____

_____ _____

_____ _____

_____ _____

_____ _____

turn the page

VOCABULARY (continued)

_____   _____

_____   _____

_____   _____

_____   _____

_____   _____

_____   _____

_____   _____

_____   _____

_____   _____

_____   _____

_____   _____

Unit 2

Letters, Sounds, Abbreviations, Spelling, and Alphabetizing

Unit 2

Letters, Sounds, Abbreviations, Spelling, and Alphabetizing

The emphasis in this unit is on the letters and sounds of English. The goals of the unit are:

    . . . to give practice with letters and sounds

    . . . to provide vocabulary words and phrases used in discussing them

    . . . to present a little information about English spelling and pronunciation.

Be sure to ask questions and discuss the unit with your teacher.

Most of the lessons are quite short. Few are over five minutes of writing time. The first part of the unit contains three *Review Lessons*. All three are easy. During these lessons please take time to improve your printing of English letters and your writing of English letters. (Refer to the reference sheets on pages 51 and 52.) The second part of the unit contains eight *Context Lessons*. These include practical work in aural spelling (and oral spelling), matching sounds and spellings, and abbreviations. The concepts of initials, acronyms, homonyms, and "spoken" abbreviations are explained. The third part of the unit contains seven *Problem Lessons* with realistic uses of letters which will help you in your studies. These include translating Roman numerals, alphabetizing, rhyming, spelling rules, and pronunciation-spelling correspondences. (Refer to the reference sheets on pages 87 and 88.) The last two lessons are word-game *Test Lessons*.

ALPHABET SYSTEM

The alphabet we use today can be traced back in time for nearly four thousand years. It has had many changes since its early origin in the Middle East. As this chart shows, we can trace the development of the alphabet from Semitic to Phoenician to Greek to Latin to English. The word "alphabet" comes from the Greek forms of the Semitic names of the two letters "alpha" and "beta."

Hebrew letter	Hebrew letter name	Phoenician letter	Greek letter	Greek letter name	Latin letter	English letter
Ӿ	aleph	Ϟ	⍺	alpha	A	A
٦	beth	⌂	β	beta	B	B

Listen carefully. Print the letter you hear — *both* **the** *capital* **letter and the** *small* **letter. Put one letter on each line.**

Group 1		*Group 2*	
capital	*small*	*capital*	*small*
_____	_____	_____	_____
_____	_____	_____	_____
_____	_____	_____	_____
_____	_____	_____	_____
_____	_____	_____	_____
_____	_____	_____	_____
_____	_____	_____	_____
_____	_____	_____	_____
_____	_____	_____	_____
_____	_____	_____	_____
_____	_____	_____	_____

AURAL COMPREHENSION QUESTIONS

Listen to each question carefully.

1. _____

2. _____

3. _____

4. _____

DISCUSSION TOPICS

1. Uses of capitals and small letters.

2. Vowels and consonants.

3. Contrast printed and written letters.

VOCABULARY AND PRONUNCIATION

Practice aloud. Discuss meanings.

vowels	Semitic
consonants	Hebrew
written language	Phoenician
letters	Greek
spoken language	Latin
sounds	English
_____	Middle East
printed form	_____
capital letter	alpha
upper case	beta
small letter	alphabet
lower case	alphabetical order
_____	alphabetize
trace	
origin	

50

LETTERS — PRINTED FORMS*

This is a reference sheet for the printed forms of capital letters (upper case) and small letters (lower case).

Use this as a reference sheet. Practice printing.

Aa   Bb   Cc   Dd   Ee

Ff   Gg   Hh   Ii   Jj

Kk   Ll   Mm   Nn   Oo

Pp   Qq   Rr   Ss   Tt

Uu   Vv   Ww   Xx   Yy   Zz

---

*Notice the differences:
  1. Printed Letters
  2. *Written Letters*
  3. BLOCK LETTERS

LETTERS — WRITTEN (CURSIVE) FORMS

This is a reference sheet for the cursive forms of capital letters and small letters. The cursive form is the form of writing in which the strokes of the letters are joined in each word. It is often more difficult than the printed form for second language learners. These letters are from a penmanship method* taught in many schools. You may find it somewhat different from other methods of handwriting. Some of you may be confused because you have been taught a method based on Greek written letters.

It is suggested that you practice each letter so that you learn to recognize it. You do not need to change your penmanship if you have learned other forms but you should learn to recognize these forms.

Aa Bb Cc Dd Ee

Ff Gg Hh Ii Jj

Kk Ll Mm Nn Oo

Pp Qq Rr Ss Tt

Uu Vv Ww Xx Yy Zz

*Palmer Method

RECOGNIZING AND PRONOUNCING LETTER NAMES

English has letter names which differ from those used in other languages although the letter itself is exactly the same. For example, English calls the letter *B* by the name "bee" but Spanish calls the letter *B* by the letter name "bay." Be sure you do not confuse the letter names used by different languages. Letters which have similar patterns of pronunciation have been grouped together.

Listen carefully. Print the capital letter. Put one letter on each line.

Letter   *Letter*

Group #1   Group #4

_____   _____

_____   _____

_____   _____

Group #2   Group #5

_____   _____

_____   _____

_____   _____

_____   _____

_____   _____

_____ Group #6 — Miscellaneous

_____   _____

_____   _____

Group #3   _____

_____

_____

AURAL COMPREHENSION QUESTIONS

Listen to each question carefully.

1. _____

2. _____

3. _____

DISCUSSION TOPICS

1. Patterns of pronunciation in Groups 1 through 6.

2. Phonetic spelling (see list below).

3. The following pairs confuse some students. Why?

C – Z	L – R	M – N	B – P	S – X
B – V	D – B	G – J	V – W	I – E – A

VOCABULARY AND PRONUNCIATION

Practice aloud. Discuss meanings.

letter names	differ from	pronunciation
rhyme	similar	patterns

Reference

PHONETIC SPELLING OF THE ENGLISH LETTER NAMES*

A	/e/	F	/ɛf/	K	/ke/	P	/pi/	U	/yu/
B	/bi/	G	/dʒi/	L	/ɛl/	Q	/kyu/	V	/vi/
C	/si/	H	/etʃ/	M	/ɛm/	R	/ar/	W	/dəblyu/
D	/di/	I	/aI/	N	/ɛn/	S	/ɛs/	X	/ɛks/
E	/i/	J	/dʒe/	O	/o/	T	/ti/	Y	/waI/
								Z	/zi/

———

*as pronounced in General American

ORAL SPELLING: WORDS FOR REFERENCE

"What letter did you say? I didn't understand you."

If someone doesn't understand the letter you say, give a word for reference. For example: "I said *A,* as in apple," or "I said *M,* as in mother."

Listen carefully. Write the letter. Then write the word which the teacher spells.

	Letter	*Word*		*Letter*	*Word*
1.	_____	_____	14.	_____	_____
2.	_____	_____	15.	_____	_____
3.	_____	_____	16.	_____	_____
4.	_____	_____	17.	_____	_____
5.	_____	_____	18.	_____	_____
6.	_____	_____	19.	_____	_____
7.	_____	_____	20.	_____	_____
8.	_____	_____	21.	_____	_____
9.	_____	_____	22.	_____	_____
10.	_____	_____	23.	_____	_____
11.	_____	_____	24.	_____	_____
12.	_____	_____	25.	_____	_____
13.	_____	_____	26.	_____	_____

AURAL COMPREHENSION QUESTIONS

Listen to each question carefully.

1. _____

2. _____

3. _____

DISCUSSION TOPIC

1. Code words below.

   (Practice students' names using the code below.)

VOCABULARY AND PRONUNCIATION

Practice aloud. Discuss meanings.

reference   oral spelling   A as in apple

_____

Reference

INTERNATIONAL CODE

A	as in Adams	J	as in James	S	as in Susan
B	as in Baker	K	as in King	T	as in Thomas
C	as in Charlie	L	as in Lewis	U	as in Union
D	as in David	M	as in Mary	V	as in Victor
E	as in Edward	N	as in Nancy	W	as in Williams
F	as in Frank	O	as in Otto	X	as in X-ray
G	as in George	P	as in Peter	Y	as in Yankee
H	as in Henry	Q	as in Queen	Z	as in Zebra
I	as in Ida	R	as in Robert		

(these are often used by telephone operators)

INITIALS

"What are initials? What does NBC mean? What does CIA mean?"

Abbreviated forms of names are common in many languages. The ones in this lesson are common ones used in American English.

Listen carefully. Put the initials in capital letters, printed form, and no periods between them. Work as rapidly as you can.

Column 1   *Column 2*

1. _____ – _____   a.   American Federation of Labor–Congress of Industrial Organizations

2. _____ and _____   b.   American Telephone and Telegraph

3. _____   c.   Central Intelligence Agency

4. _____   d.   Columbia Broadcasting System

5. _____   e.   Federal Bureau of Investigation

6. _____   f.   General Electric

7. _____   g.   General Motors

8. _____   h.   International Business Machines

9. _____   i.   Massachusetts Institute of Technology

10. _____   j.   National Broadcasting Company

11. _____   k.   Organization of American States

12. _____   l.   Scandinavian Air Service

13. _____   m.   United Auto Workers

14. _____   n.   University of California at Los Angeles

15. _____   o.   United Nations

16. _____   p.   United States of America

17. _____   q.   United States Information Service

18. _____   r.   Union of Soviet Socialist Republics

19. _____   s.   Volkswagen

20. _____   t.   Young Men's Christian Association

Before going to the Aural Comprehension Questions, pronounce each item in Columns 1 and 2 with your teacher. Then, in Column 2, underline each letter which appears in the abbreviation.

AURAL COMPREHENSION QUESTIONS

Listen to each question carefully.

1. _____

2. _____

3. _____

4. _____

DISCUSSION TOPICS

1. Discuss the abbreviations in the lesson and those below. Add to this list:

    VA   (Veterans' Administration)
    WHO   (World Health Organization)

    Use English language newspapers.

2. Discuss the different categories such as colleges, companies, countries, clubs, government agencies, international organizations, etc.

3. Famous people: JFK, FDR.

VOCABULARY AND PRONUNCIATION

Practice aloud. Discuss meanings.

American Federation of Labor -
   Congress of Industrial Organizations

American Telephone and Telegraph

Central Intelligence Agency

Columbia Broadcasting System

Federal Bureau of Investigation

General Electric

General Motors

International Business Machines

Massachusetts Institute of Technology

National Broadcasting Company

Organization of American States

Scandinavian Air Service

United Auto Workers

University of California at Los Angeles

United Nations

United States of America

United States Information Service

Union of Soviet Socialist Republics

Volkswagen

Young Men's Christian Association

_____

initials

abbreviated form

ACRONYMS

"What is NATO? What is radar? Are they words?"

Both are acronyms. An acronym is a word formed from the first (or first few) letters of several words. NATO, from *North Atlantic Treaty Organization*, is an example. The word radar, from *radio detecting and ranging*, is another example. The individual names of the letters are not pronounced in acronyms — as they were in the previous lesson. Spoken English makes use of many acronyms which you must be able to recognize instantly.

Listen carefully. Write the letters in capitals, except for #5 and #8. Print, with no periods between letters. Work as rapidly as you can.

Column 1		*Column 2*
1. _____	a.	Agency for International Development
2. _____	b.	Cooperative for American Relief Everywhere
3. _____	c.	Housing and Urban Development
4. _____	d.	International Police
5. _____	e.	light amplification by stimulated emission of radiation
6. _____	f.	National Aeronautics and Space Administration
7. _____	g.	North Atlantic Treaty Organization
8. _____	h.	radio detecting and ranging
9. _____	i.	Southeast Asia Treaty Organization
10. _____	j.	Strategic Air Command
11. _____	k.	Strategic Arms Limitation Talks
12. _____	l.	Supreme Headquarters, Allied Powers, Europe
13. _____	m.	United Nations Educational, Scientific, and Cultural Organization
14. _____	n.	United Nations International Children's Emergency Fund
15. _____	o.	Volunteers in Service to America

Before going to the Aural Comprehension Questions, pronounce each item in Columns 1 and 2 with your teacher. Then, in Column 2, underline each letter which appears in the acronym.

AURAL COMPREHENSION QUESTIONS

Listen to each question carefully.

1. _____

2. _____

3. _____

4. _____

DISCUSSION TOPICS

1. Discuss the acronyms in this lesson (especially the way each is formed). Add to this list:

        sonar   (**so**und **na**vigation **r**anging)

        SUNOCO   (**Sun** **O**il **Co**mpany)

2. Discuss the categories of the organizations – national, international, regional, etc.

VOCABULARY AND PRONUNCIATION

Practice aloud. Discuss meanings.

acronym	radio detecting and ranging
Agency for International Development	Southeast Asia Treaty Organization
Cooperative for American Relief Everywhere	Strategic Air Command
Housing and Urban Development (Department of)	Strategic Arms Limitation Talks
International Police	Supreme Headquarters, Allied Powers, Europe
light amplification by stimulated emission of radiation	United Nations Educational, Scientific, and Cultural Organization
National Aeronautics and Space Administration	United Nations International Children's Emergency Fund
North Atlantic Treaty Organization	Volunteers in Service to America

HOMONYMS

"What's a homonym?"

A homonym is a word with the same pronunciation as another word, but with a different meaning, origin, and spelling.

For example: no – know
pair – pear

This lesson is for rapid recognition of homonym spellings.

Listen carefully. Listen to the spelling. Look at the two choices. Circle the one the teacher spelled.

1.	made	maid		14.	wait	weight
2.	rode	road		15.	real	reel
3.	meet	meat		16.	for	four
4.	threw	through		17.	pear	pair
5.	write	right		18.	seen	scene
6.	bee	be		19.	bear	bare
7.	sea	see		20.	night	knight
8.	knot	not		21.	reed	read /rid/
9.	one	won		22.	red	read /r ɛ d/
10.	fair	fare		23.	led	lead
11.	no	know		24.	hear	here
12.	sew	so		25.	there	their
13.	two	too		26.	way	weigh

AURAL COMPREHENSION QUESTIONS

Listen to each question carefully.

1. _____

2. _____

3. _____

4. _____

DISCUSSION TOPICS

1. Meanings of these words.

2. Make a list of additional homonyms as: buy — by

    wee — we

VOCABULARY AND PRONUNCIATION

Practice aloud. Discuss meanings.

see	sea		for	four
road	rode		know	no
right	write		through	threw
meet	meat		bare	bear
won	one		bee	be
two	too		fare	fair
maid	made		hear	here
weigh	way		led	lead
seen	scene		night	knight
so	sew		not	knot
their	there		pair	pear
wait	weight		read	red
reed	read		reel	real

HOMONYMS: TRAVEL CONTEXT

"Should I spell it 'bee' or 'be'? 'For' or 'four'?"

This is the same group of homonyms we spelled in the last lesson. See if you can use them correctly in context.

Fill in the blanks.

1. In Yellowstone Park, a big _____ frightened the tourists.

2. She was stung by a _____ .

3. How much is the _____ to Paris?

4. I want _____ tickets to Amsterdam.

5. The taxi is _____ .

6. The guide _____ us into the Pyramids.

7. I want to take a _____ train to Munich.

8. The sailor tied a _____ in the rope.

9. I don't _____ which train to take.

10. We went to _____ the President of Mexico.

11. He _____ a trip to Japan.

12. I want a _____ of tickets to Madrid.

13. The _____ poppies were blooming in Greece.

14. I _____ a camel in Egypt.

15. The Mediterranean _____ is clear and blue.

16. Many passengers _____ their newspapers on the subway.

17. The sky in Turkey is always _____ clear and bright.

18. _____ luggage was delivered.

19. I want _____ tickets to Rome.

20. What is the _____ of your luggage?

21. Is this the _____ road to Berlin?

22. They _____ the Grand Prix.

AURAL COMPREHENSION QUESTIONS

Listen to each question carefully.

1. _____

2. _____

3. _____

4. _____

DISCUSSION TOPICS

1. Discuss your spelling mistakes.

2. Discuss the travel vocabulary.

VOCABULARY AND PRONUNCIATION

Practice aloud. Discuss meanings.

Paris	Turkey	poppies
Amsterdam	Rome	blooming
Pyramids	New York	camel
Munich	Berlin	subway
Mexico	Grand Prix	luggage
Japan	Yellowstone Park	tourists
Madrid	tickets	frightened
Greece	taxi	a big bear
Egypt	guide	stung by a bee
Mediterranean Sea	train	

ORAL SPELLING: MEDICAL CONTEXT

"How do you spell it?"

Certain words are especially difficult to spell in English. Here are the twenty which are misspelled most often by native speakers.

Listen carefully. Write the word as it is spelled.

1. He has_____ many colds each winter.

2. The children had _____ vaccinations in November.

3. Medicine loses _____ strength if it is kept too long.

4. Many people _____ health insurance is essential.

5. Older people _____ health care through Medicare.

6. A cholera epidemic _____ in India in 1971.

7. The _____ use of drugs is as pain-killer.

8. There are _____ wards for contagious diseases.

9. The first heart transplant was a historic _____ .

10. Medicine must not _____ in its battle to conquer cancer.

11. _____ are many famous doctors in Switzerland.

12. _____ vaccines were discovered, many people died of polio.

13. Tetanus and smallpox shots are often given _____ .

14. The _____ of air pollution is dangerous to health.

15. The Mayo Clinic has always _____ in the field of medical care.

16. Call a doctor _____ if someone has a heart attack.

17. Pneumonia may _____ following surgery.

18. An accurate _____ of disease symptoms is important.

19. The _____ of hearing is called the auditory sense.

20. There is a _____ need for more doctors and nurses.

AURAL COMPREHENSION QUESTIONS

Listen to each question carefully.

1. _____

2. _____

3. _____

4. _____

DISCUSSION TOPICS

1. Discuss your spelling mistakes.

2. Discuss the medical vocabulary.

VOCABULARY AND PRONUNCIATION

Practice aloud. Discuss meanings.

believe	principal	colds	contagious
definite	receive	shots	disease
description	sense	vaccination	heart transplant
develop	separate	vaccine	cancer
existence	their	medicine	polio
immediately	there	health insurance	tetanus
its	together	health care	smallpox
led	too	Mayo Clinic	air pollution
lose	until	cholera	pneumonia
occasion	pain-killer	epidemic	surgery
occurred	auditory	drugs	symptoms

SPOKEN ABBREVIATIONS IN GENERAL USE (1)

"What did he say? What do those letters mean?"

Abbreviated forms of words and phrases are often heard in English. If you do not recognize them, you will misunderstand an entire sentence. The abbreviations in this lesson are very common in both spoken and written English.

Listen carefully. Write the following letter abbreviations as your teacher reads them. They are all combinations of letters which the teacher will spell. Work as rapidly as you can.

Column 1	*Column 2*
1. _____	a. American Automobile Association (triple A)
2. _____	b. Anno Domini (year of our Lord)
3. _____	c. ante meridiem (before noon)
4. _____	d. bachelor of arts (degree)
5. _____	e. before Christ
6. _____	f. cash on delivery
7. _____	g. dichloro-diphenyl-trichloroethane
8. _____	h. doctor of dental surgery (dentist)
9. _____	i. "I owe you." (a written note promising to pay)
10. _____	j. intelligence quotient
11. _____	k. master of arts (degree)
12. _____	l. master of ceremonies
13. _____	m. medical doctor (doctor of medicine)
14. _____	n. philosophy doctorate (doctor of philosophy)
15. _____	o. post meridiem (after noon)
16. _____	p. public address (system)
17. _____	q. registered nurse
18. _____	r. répondez s'il vous plaît" (French for "please reply")
19. _____	s. SOS signal (wireless signal for help)
20. _____	t. television
21. _____	u. tuberculosis

Before going to the Aural Comprehension Questions, pronounce each item in Columns 1 and 2 with your teacher. Then, in Column 2, underline each letter which appears in the abbreviation.

67

AURAL COMPREHENSION QUESTIONS

Listen to each question carefully.

1. _____

2. _____

3. _____

4. _____

DISCUSSION TOPICS

†1. Discuss these abbreviations. Add to the list.

2. Discuss the different categories, such as college degrees, dates, times, etc.

3. Discuss B.A. – B.S. – M.A. – M.S. – Ph.D.

VOCABULARY AND PRONUNCIATION

Practice aloud. Discuss meanings.

stand for

abbreviate

abbreviations

American Automobile Association

Anno Domini (year of our Lord)

*ante meridiem (before noon)

bachelor of arts

before Christ

*cash on delivery

*dichloro-diphenyl-trichloroethane

doctor of dental surgery

*I owe you ____ .

*intelligence quotient

master of arts

*master of ceremonies

(doctor of) medicine

(doctor of) philosophy

*post meridiem (after noon)

*public address system

registered nurse

*répondez s'il vous plaît (French) please reply

*signal of distress (SOS)

*television

*tuberculosis

†Periods are sometimes omitted in all of these abbreviations.
*These are sometimes written in small letters.

SPOKEN ABBREVIATIONS (2)

"What did he say? What do those letters mean?"

The English language is full of abbreviated forms for common words and phrases. You will hear them and see them in print every day.

Listen carefully. Write the following letters as the teacher reads them. They will be combinations of letters. Work as rapidly as you can.

Column 1	*Column 2*
1. _____	a. absent without official leave
2. _____	b. Alcoholics Anonymous
3. _____	c. amplitude modulation (sound transmission)
4. _____	d. anti-ballistic missile
5. _____	e. Army Post Office
6. _____	f. certified public accountant
7. _____	g. frequency modulation (sound transmission)
8. _____	h. government issue
9. _____	i. Health, Education, and Welfare Department
10. _____	j. identification (card)
11. _____	k. intercontinental ballistic missile
12. _____	l. military police (policeman)
13. _____	m. Parent-Teachers' Association
14. _____	n. postscript
15. _____	o. prisoner of war
16. _____	p. private first class
17. _____	q. supersonic transport (airliner)
18. _____	r. ultra-high frequency (sound transmission)
19. _____	s. very high frequency (sound transmission)
20. _____	t. very important person

Before going to the Aural Comprehension Questions, pronounce each item in Columns 1 and 2 with your teacher. Then, in Column 2, underline each letter which appears in the abbreviation.

> SUGGESTION: After this lesson you may wish to begin work on Unit Three (page 95) and alternate lessons from Units Two and Three.

AURAL COMPREHENSION QUESTIONS

Listen to each question carefully.

1. _____

2. _____

3. _____

4. _____

DISCUSSION TOPICS

†1. Discuss these abbreviations. Add to the list.

2. Discuss the categories.

3. Consult a newspaper for uses of abbreviations.

VOCABULARY AND PRONUNCIATION

Practice aloud. Discuss meanings.

common words and phrases

see them in print

abbreviated forms

*absent without official leave

Alcoholics Anonymous

*amplitude modulation

*anti-ballistic missile

Army Post Office

*certified public accountant

*frequency modulation

*government issue

Health, Education, and Welfare Department

*identification (card)

*intercontinental ballistic missile

*military police

Parent-Teacher Association

*postscript

*prisoner of war

*private first class

*supersonic transport

*ultra-high frequency

*very high frequency

*very important person

---

†Periods are sometimes omitted in all of these abbreviations.
*These are sometimes written in small letters.

SCIENCE ABBREVIATIONS

"How do you spell it? How do you abbreviate it?"

It is important to know the spelling and abbreviation of the following scientific terms.

Listen carefully. Write each abbreviation as the teacher spells it. Write small letters, unless the teacher indicates capitals, and no periods.

Abbreviation	*Full Spelling*
1. _____	a. alternating current
2. _____	b. boiling point
3. _____	c. British thermal unit
4. _____	d. centimeter-gram-second (system)
5. _____	e. chemically pure
6. _____	f. counter electromotive force
7. _____	g. cubic feet per second
8. _____	h. cycles per second
9. _____	i. degrees Centigrade
10. _____	j. degrees Fahrenheit
11. _____	k. direct current
12. _____	l. electromotive force
13. _____	m. foot-pound-second (system)
14. _____	n. freezing point
15. _____	o. horsepower
16. _____	p. kilowatt hour
17. _____	q. miles per hour
18. _____	r. parts per million
19. _____	s. revolutions per minute
20. _____	t. tensile strength

AURAL COMPREHENSION QUESTIONS

Listen to each question carefully.

1. _____

2. _____

3. _____

4. _____

DISCUSSION TOPIC

1. Discuss these abbreviations. Add to the list.

VOCABULARY AND PRONUNCIATION

Practice aloud. Discuss meanings.

alternating current	direct current
British thermal unit	electromotive force
boiling point	foot-pound-second (system)
centimeter-gram-second (system)	freezing point
chemically pure	horsepower
counter electromotive force	kilowatt hour
cubic feet per second	miles per hour
cycles per second	parts per million
degrees Centigrade	revolutions per minute
degrees Fahrenheit	tensile strength

ROMAN NUMERALS

"What are the Roman numerals? What does XXX mean?"

The values of 7 letters and 5 general rules make up this system:

Letters: I = 1   V = 5   X = 10   L = 50   C = 100   D = 500   M = 1000

Rules: (1)   Repeating a letter repeats its value (XX = 20).
        (2)   A letter placed *after* one of greater value *adds* to its value (VI = 6).
        (3)   A letter placed *before* one of greater value *subtracts* from its value (IV = 4).
        (4)   A bar over a numeral *multiplies* the value by 1000 ($\overline{X}$ = 10,000).
        (5)   Always read Roman numerals from left to right.

Write capital letters.

	Roman Numeral	*Arabic Number*
1. Chapter	_____	_____
2. Chapter	_____	_____
3. Chapter	_____	_____
4. Chapter	_____	_____
5. In the year	_____	_____
6. In the year	_____	_____
7. In the year	_____	_____
8. In the year	_____	_____
*9. Henry	_____ th	_____
*10. Louis	_____ th	_____
*11. Elizabeth	_____ th	_____
*12. King George	_____ th	_____
13. In the _____ th Century B.C.		_____
14. In the _____ st Century A.D.		_____
15. In the _____ th Century B.C.		_____
16. In the _____ th Century A.D.		_____
17. Chemical Group #	_____	_____
18. Chemical Group #	_____	_____
19. Chemical Group #	_____	_____
20. Chemical Group #	_____	_____

*In speaking, *the* is sometimes added – as: "Henry (the) VIIth."

PROBLEM

Using this page as a reference sheet, translate the Roman numerals you have just written into Arabic numbers. Work as rapidly as you can.

DISCUSSION TOPIC

1. Reading Roman numerals.

VOCABULARY AND PRONUNCIATION

Practice aloud. Discuss meanings.

Roman numerals   Arabic numerals

Reference			ROMAN NUMERALS				
1	... I	11	... XI	30	... XXX	400	... CD
2	... II	12	... XII	40	... XL	500	... D
3	... III	13	... XIII	50	... L	600	... DC
4	... IV	14	... XIV	60	... LX	700	... DCC
5	... V	15	... XV	70	... LXX	800	... DCCC
6	... VI	16	... XVI	80	... LXXX	900	... CM
7	... VII	17	... XVII	90	... XC	1000	... M
8	... VIII	18	... XVIII	100	... C	1900	... MCM
9	... IX	19	... XIX	200	... CC	2000	... MM
10	... X	20	... XX	300	... CCC	5000	... $\overline{V}$

ENGLISH FAMILY NAMES: ALPHABETIZING

"How do you spell your name?"

It is important to know how to spell some of the family names (i.e., surnames or last names) used frequently in English speaking countries. The surnames in this lesson are the fifteen most common names in the United States.

Listen carefully. Spell the name as the teacher dictates. Work as rapidly as you can.

Column 1: Dictated List	*Column 2: Alphabetized List*
1. _____	_____
2. _____	_____
3. _____	_____
4. _____	_____
5. _____	_____
6. _____	_____
7. _____	_____
8. _____	_____
9. _____	_____
10. _____	_____
11. _____	_____
12. _____	_____
13. _____	_____
14. _____	_____
15. _____	_____

PROBLEM

Alphabetize these names as quickly as you can. That is, put these names in alphabetical order as they should appear in an alphabetized list — such as in the telephone book. Ask your teacher for help if necessary.

DISCUSSION TOPICS

1. Discuss common family names and the form "The Browns."

2. Make a list of common English given names such as:

    Robert
    David
    Mary
    Susan

3. Titles and signatures (i.e., Mrs., Miss, Mr.).

4. Nicknames (Robert — Bob — Bobby).

VOCABULARY AND PRONUNCIATION

Practice aloud. Discuss meanings.

last name

surname

family name

first name

given name

maiden name

nickname

Reference

MOST FREQUENT U.S. GIVEN NAMES

Male		*Female*	
John	George	Mary	Betty
William	Willie	Dorothy	Elizabeth
James	Joseph	Helen	Anna
Robert	Frank	Margaret	Mildred
Charles	Richard	Ruth	Frances

SPELLING GUIDES (1)

"How do you spell it? What spelling rule will help me?"

Here are two spelling rules to help you. Remember, however, there are often exceptions to rules.

Listen carefully. Read the rule as the teacher reads it. Then practice as the teacher dictates.

Rule A: If a verb ends in *y* preceded by a consonant, CHANGE the *y* to *i* and add *-ed* to form the regular past tense form.*
(Example: bury — buried)

1. _____   _____   5. _____   _____

2. _____   _____   6. _____   _____

3. _____   _____   7. _____   _____

4. _____   _____   8. _____   _____

Rule B: If a verb is one syllable (OR is accented on the *last* syllable) and ends in a single consonant preceded by a single short vowel, DOUBLE the final consonant and add *-ing*† to make the progressive form.
(Example: hop — hopping)

1. _____   _____   5. _____   _____

2. _____   _____   6. _____   _____

3. _____   _____   7. _____   _____

4. _____   _____   8. _____   _____

---

*This rule can be expanded to include noun, adjective, and adverb suffixing as in *babies, prettier, lazily,* etc.
†This rule also applies to other suffixes which begin with vowels. (See page 78.)

PROBLEM

Find *four* more examples for each spelling rule in this lesson. Write them here. Ask your teacher for help if necessary.

DISCUSSION TOPICS

1. Discuss these rules and possible expansions.

2. Discuss short vowels and the doubling rule for suffixes beginning with vowels (see list below).

3. Discuss the pronunciation of these pairs: cūter – cŭtter;   hōping – hŏpping.*

VOCABULARY AND PRONUNCIATION

base word	spelling guides	short vowels (lax vowels)
derived word	exceptions	long vowels (tense vowels)

Reference

SOME SHORT (LAX) ENGLISH VOWELS

ĭ	ĕ	ŭ	ŏ	ă
hit	set	run	rob	fat
hitting	setting	runner	robber	fatten
big	red	sun	hop	wrap
biggest	redden	sunny	hopping	wrapper
begin	regret	nut	stop	chat
beginner	regretted	nutty	stopper	chatter

SOME SUFFIXES BEGINNING WITH VOWELS

-ing   -er   -est   -en   -y   -ant   -ous

---

*Pronounce with a long vowel before a single consonant and a short vowel before a double consonant in medial position. For homework find more examples.

78

SPELLING GUIDES (2)

"How do you spell it? What spelling rule will help me?"

Here are two more spelling rules to help you. Remember, however, there are often exceptions to rules.

Listen carefully. Read the rule as the teacher reads it. Then practice as the teacher dictates.

Rule C: *To form regular plurals add *-es* and pronounce as an extra syllable if the word ends in *s, ss, zz, ch, sh,* or *x.*†

(Example: watch — watches)

1. _____   _____   5. _____   _____

2. _____   _____   6. _____   _____

3. _____   _____   7. _____   _____

4. _____   _____   8. _____   _____

Rule D: If a word ends in a silent *e* preceded by a consonant or *y* DROP the *e* before adding a suffix beginning with a vowel.

(Example: fame — famous)

1. _____   _____   5. _____   _____

2. _____   _____   6. _____   _____

3. _____   _____   7. _____   _____

4. _____   _____   8. _____   _____

---

*This rule also is used to form the third person singular form of regular verbs.
†If a word ends in *se, ze, dge* or *ge*, add only *-s* but pronounce as an extra syllable.

PROBLEM

Please find *four* more examples for each spelling rule in this lesson. Write them here. Ask your teacher for help if necessary.

DISCUSSION TOPIC

1. Discuss these rules and possible expansions.

VOCABULARY AND PRONUNCIATION

Practice aloud. Discuss meanings.

suffix   regular

preceded by   plural

PRONOUNCING VOWEL PAIRS: TENSE and LAX (LONG and SHORT)

The vowels in *chīld* and *wīld* sound like long *ī* while the vowels in *chĭldren* and *wĭlderness* sound like the sound in *ĭt* (short *i*). Let us list this and four other pairs of related vowels. For each pair of vowel sounds many words* can be found which follow the pronunciation change.

Write the words as they are read.

Group 1: 1. _____ _____   Group 4: 1. _____ _____

2. _____ _____   2. _____ _____

3. _____ _____   3. _____ _____

4. _____ _____   4. _____ _____

Group 2: 1. _____ _____   Group 5: 1. _____ _____

2. _____ _____   2. _____ _____

3. _____ _____   3. _____ _____

4. _____ _____   4. _____ _____

Group 3: 1. _____ _____

2. _____ _____

3. _____ _____

4. _____ _____

_____

*See page 87 for more examples. Students may want to study page 87 before doing this lesson.

PROBLEM

_____

_____

_____

_____

Ask your teacher for help if necessary. Study the reference sheet on page 87.

DISCUSSION TOPICS

1. Discuss these groups of vowels.

2. Find more examples.

VOCABULARY AND PRONUNCIATION

Practice aloud. Discuss meanings.

vowel pairs   related vowels

long vowels, tense vowels   pronunciation change

short vowels, lax vowels

| divīde | plēase | redūce | cōne | nātion |
| divĭsion | plĕasant | redŭction | cŏnical | nătionality |

RHYMING (1)

"What does rhyme mean? Do words have to be spelled alike in order to rhyme?"

Two words rhyme when the last sounds of the words are the same.* This must include the *accented* vowel PLUS the remainder of each word. Words do NOT have to be *spelled* alike in order to rhyme; they must be *pronounced* alike. For example:

(f)éet	(m)óney	(m)ótion
(m)eát	(f)únny	ócean

Write two KEY words for each group as the teacher spells them.

Group 1 _____   Group 4 _____

_____   _____

_____   _____

Group 2 _____   Group 5 _____

_____   _____

_____   _____

Group 3 _____   Group 6 _____

_____   _____

_____   _____

_____

*See page 88 for examples. Students may want to study page 88 before doing this lesson.

PROBLEM

_____

_____

_____

_____

Ask your teacher for help if necessary. Study the reference sheet on rhyming and common spellings for sounds (page 88).

DISCUSSION TOPICS

1. Discuss the common ways of spelling different sounds (see reference sheet).

2. Make up a list of several-syllable rhyming words.

(v)ánity	(ch)éerily	(con)fúsion
(s)ánity	(w)éarily	(de)lúsion

VOCABULARY AND PRONUNCIATION

Practice aloud. Discuss meanings.

rhyme

rhyming

sound alike

pronounced alike

accented vowel

remainder

RHYMING (2)

"What does rhyme mean? Do words have to be spelled alike in order to rhyme?"

Two words rhyme when the last sounds of the words are the same.* This must include the *accented* vowel PLUS the remainder of each word. Words do NOT have to be *spelled* alike in order to rhyme; they must be *pronounced* alike. For example:

(t)óe	(l)óve	(ch)ánger
(sn)ów	(a)bóve	(r)ánger

Write two KEY words for each group as the teacher spells them.

Group 1 _____   Group 4 _____

_____   _____

_____   _____

Group 2 _____   Group 5 _____

_____   _____

_____   _____

Group 3 _____   Group 6 _____

_____   _____

_____   _____

*See page 88 for examples. Students may want to study page 88 before doing this lesson.

PROBLEM

_____

_____

_____

_____

Ask your teacher for help if necessary. Discuss rhyming. Study the reference sheet on rhyming and common spellings for sounds (page 88).

DISCUSSION TOPICS

1. Discuss rhyming.

2. Make up a list of difficult rhyming words.

VOCABULARY AND PRONUNCIATION

Practice aloud. Discuss meanings.

(all the words in Lessons 17 and 18)

PRONUNCIATION – VOWEL PAIRS*

Group 1		**Group 4**	
ī	ĭ	ō	ŏ
five	fifth	know	knowledge
wide	width	cone	conical
wise	wisdom	holy	holiday
decide	decision	mode	modify
dine	dinner	phone	phonic
crime	criminal	tone	tonic
type	typical		

Group 2		**Group 5**	
ē	ĕ	ā	ă
please	pleasant	nation	national
sleep	slept	Spain	Spanish
deceive	deception	insane	insanity
convene	convention	explain	explanatory
meter	metric	grade	gradual
heal	health	nature	natural

Group 3	
ū	ŭ
produce	production
youth	young
consume	consumption
student	study
judicial	judge

————

*Many more pairs of words can be found in the English language for each of these groups. However, not all pairs in the groups follow the pronunciation Aural change for the same linguistic reason. The purpose of this reference sheet and the content of Lesson 16 is merely to call attention to this phenomenon of English pronunciation.

RHYMING — VOWEL SPELLING EXAMPLES*

Vowel 1

feet
meat

fee
key
she
ski

machine
between

Vowel 2

hit
mitt
quit

build
filled

Vowel 3

plane
Spain
rain

say
gray
they

Vowel 4

bed
dead
said

guess
less
yes

Vowel 5

cat
flat
sat

laugh
half

Vowel 6

won
run

much
touch

cuff
rough

Vowel 7

top
stop
pop

collar
dollar

bar
car

Vowel 8

blue
too
do
knew

cool
rule

fruit
boot
suit

Vowel 9

book
took

wool
full

could
would
wood

Vowel 10

ocean
motion

boat
vote

no
snow
though
foe

Vowel 11

law
saw

talk
walk

thought
taught

Diphthong 1

tie
sigh
my
eye

bite
right

Diphthong 2

loud
crowd

brown
noun

Diphthong 3

joy
boy

voice
rejoice

---

*The purpose of this reference sheet and the contents of Lessons 17 and 18 is not to attempt to teach spelling. The purpose is to call attention to some of the differences in spelling patterns for different sounds.

SCRAMBLED LETTERS: COUNTRIES

"What letter? Please repeat the letters."

The name of each country is all mixed up — in scrambled order. See if you can unscramble each and put the letters in the correct order.

Listen carefully. Write down each group of letters as the teacher dictates.

Scrambled Letters	*Name of the Country*
1. _____	_____
2. _____	_____
3. _____	_____
4. _____	_____
5. _____	_____
6. _____	_____
7. _____	_____
8. _____	_____
9. _____	_____
10. _____	_____
11. _____	_____
12. _____	_____
13. _____	_____
14. _____	_____
15. _____	_____
16. _____	_____

TEST

What is the name of each country?

Ask your teacher for *clues* if necessary.

DISCUSSION TOPICS

1. Discuss the geographical location of each country.

2. Make up a similar test for your fellow students.

VOCABULARY AND PRONUNCIATION

Practice aloud.

(all the names of countries in this lesson)

scrambled order

unscramble

SCRAMBLED LETTERS: WORLD CITIES

"What letter? Please repeat the letters."

The name of each city is all mixed up — in scrambled order. See if you can unscramble each and put the letters in the correct order.

Listen carefully. Write down each group of letters as the teacher dictates.

Scrambled Letters   *Name of the City*

1. _____   _____

2. _____   _____

3. _____   _____

4. _____   _____

5. _____   _____

6. _____   _____

7. _____   _____

8. _____   _____

9. _____   _____

10. _____   _____

11. _____   _____

12. _____   _____

13. _____   _____

14. _____   _____

15. _____   _____

16. _____   _____

TEST

What is the name of each city?

Ask your teacher for *clues* if necessary.

DISCUSSION TOPICS

1. Discuss the geographical location of each city and its country.

2. Make up a similar test for your fellow students.

VOCABULARY AND PRONUNCIATION

Practice aloud.

(all the names of cities in this lesson)

VOCABULARY LIST
LETTERS, SPELLING, AND ALPHABETICAL RELATIONSHIPS

Write your personal list of new words. Review this list and be sure you know each vocabulary item.

_____   _____

_____   _____

_____   _____

_____   _____

_____   _____

_____   _____

_____   _____

_____   _____

_____   _____

_____   _____

_____   _____

_____   _____

_____   _____

turn the page

VOCABULARY (continued)

_____   _____

_____   _____

_____   _____

_____   _____

_____   _____

_____   _____

_____   _____

_____   _____

_____   _____

_____   _____

_____   _____

_____   _____

_____   _____

_____   _____

_____   _____

_____   _____

Unit 3
Directions and Spatial Relations

Unit 3

Directions and Spatial Relations

Understanding directions and space relationships is often one of the most difficult parts of language learning. Much of the meaning of these phrases is relative, not absolute. Instant understanding is essential for good aural comprehension. This unit presents review and practice in basic directions, space concepts, and geographical relationships. Do not hesitate to ask questions and discuss the unit with your teacher. The goals of the unit are:

... to provide practice with directional and spatial relationships

... to present some practical use of charts, graphs, maps, and geographical locations.

In addition, special emphasis in this unit is given to the difficult task of *following aural directions.* Many students have requested practice in this area.

These lessons are a little longer than those in Units 1 and 2. As you might expect, they are also a little harder than previous lessons. Several of the lessons combine material learned in the other two units.

The first part of the unit contains six *Review Lessons.* It is very important that you understand the vocabulary in these six lessons. The second part of the unit contains six *Context Lessons*. These include charts, signs and symbols, maps, and graphs. The third part of the unit contains six *Problem Lessons* — realistic use of space and directions as you will meet them in real-life situations. Two stress geographical locations, two involve locating stores and city buildings, and two deal with arrangement of merchandise in stores. The last two lessons are quite difficult *Test Lessons.* They test memory, logic, and spatial relationships.

DIRECTIONS AND POSITIONS

One of the most difficult things to learn in a foreign language is the different ways of giving directions and describing positions. We will look at several different ways of expressing these relationships. Listen carefully to the prepositions used in many of the phrases.

Fill in the spaces as the teacher reads.

Group 1: Compass Directions

1._____

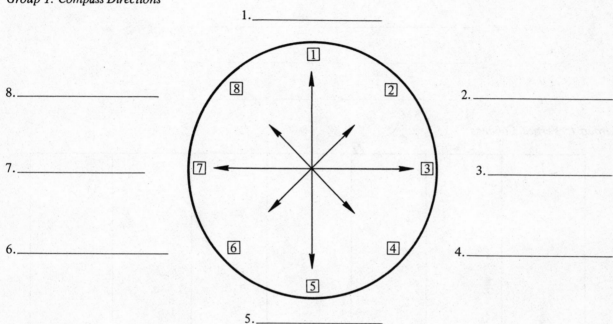

8._____

2._____

7._____

3._____

6._____

4._____

5._____

Group 2: Flat Positions

1.	2.	3. upper right
4.	5.	6.
7.	8.	9.

Group 3: Horizontal Rows (Lines)

1. _____

2. _____

    (   )

3. _____

4. _____

5. _____

6. _____

    (   )

7. _____

Group 4: Vertical Columns

1	2	3	4	5	6	7

AURAL COMPREHENSION QUESTIONS

1. _____

2. _____

3. _____

4. _____

DISCUSSION TOPIC

1. Discuss and practice these directions orally.

VOCABULARY AND PRONUNCIATION

north	south	east	west
northeast	southeast	northwest	southwest

the center	the middle	mid-central	the upper left
the upper central	the middle left	the upper right	the lower left
the lower central	the middle right	the lower right	

the top	the next to the top	the 2nd from the top	the 3rd from the top
the bottom	the next to the bottom	the 2nd from the bottom	the 3rd from the bottom

compass directions	flat positions	horizontal rows	vertical columns

the left	the 2nd one on the left
on the far left	the 2nd one from the left
the 1st one on the left	the 3rd one from the left

the right	the 2nd one on the right
on the far right	the 2nd one from the right
the 1st one on the right	the 3rd one from the right

THREE DIMENSIONS: OUTSIDE RELATIONSHIPS

"What is near? What is far?"

These words and many like them have meaning only because of the relationship of one object to another. We have used a bird and a cage to show relationships between an object *outside* another object.

Listen carefully.

1.

2.

3.

4.

5.

6.

| in back of _____ | over _____ | close to _____ |
| (behind) | (above) | (near) |

in front of _____	under _____	far away from _____
(before)	(below)	(far from)
	(underneath)	
	(beneath)	

7.

8.

9.

10.

11.

between _____   on top of _____   facing toward _____
                                     (on the top of)
                                     (on)

beside _____   facing away from _____
(next to)
(by)

AURAL COMPREHENSION QUESTIONS

1. _____

2. _____

3. _____

4. _____

DISCUSSION TOPIC

1. Discuss and practice these spatial relationships orally.

VOCABULARY AND PRONUNCIATION

before   close to
                                      ____
in front of   on
____
behind   on top of

in back of   on the top of
____   ____
under   far from

below   far away from
                                      ____
beneath   beside

underneath   by
____
over   next to
                                      ____
above   between
____   ____
facing away from   one-dimension

away from   two-dimensions
____
facing toward   three-dimensions
                                      ____
toward   exterior to (outside)

near

THREE DIMENSIONS: INSIDE RELATIONSHIPS

"What is in? What is within?"

These words and others which describe *interior* (inside) locations are sometimes difficult. The prepositions and the articles used are *very* important. Again we have used a bird and a cage to illustrate relationships of one object *inside* another.

Listen carefully.

1.

2.

3.

OUR BIRD AND CAGE AS SEEN FROM ABOVE.

4.

5. BACK

FRONT

6.

7.

8. BACK

FRONT

9.
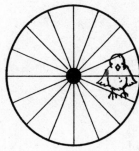

in the middle of _____   in the back of _____   on the left side of _____

in the top of _____   in the front of _____   on the right side of _____

in the bottom of _____   to one side of _____   in the center of _____

AURAL COMPREHENSION QUESTIONS

1. _____

2. _____

3. _____

4. _____

DISCUSSION TOPIC

1. Discuss this relationship and others like it:

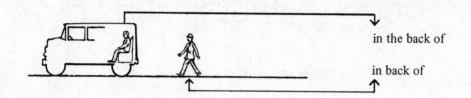

in the back of

in back of

VOCABULARY AND PRONUNCIATION

interior	to one side of
in	at the side of
inside	____
inside of	in the middle of
____	in the center of
in the top of	____
in the bottom of	on the left of
____	at the left of
in the back of	____
at the back of	on the right of
____	at the right of
in the front of	
at the front of	

FOLLOWING DIRECTIONS AND DESCRIBING RELATIONSHIPS

"Where is the post office? Where is the bank?"

Following directions in a city or town can be very difficult. Many of the phrases are confusing. The prepositions and articles are particularly important.

Listen to the directions as the teacher reads them.

Group 1

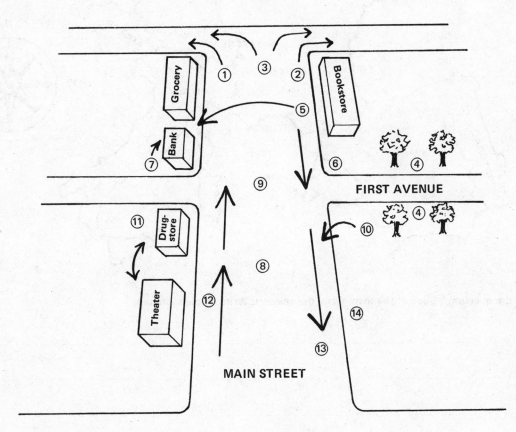

across the street _____	into the street _____
around the corner _____ (right or left)	next door to _____
at the intersection of 1st and Main _____	on both sides of the street _____
*back down the street _____	on the corner _____
beside the bank _____	turn to the right _____
in the middle of the block _____	turn to the left _____
in the middle of the street _____	*up the street _____

*Down the street = street address numbers become smaller.   Up the street = street address numbers become larger.

Group 2

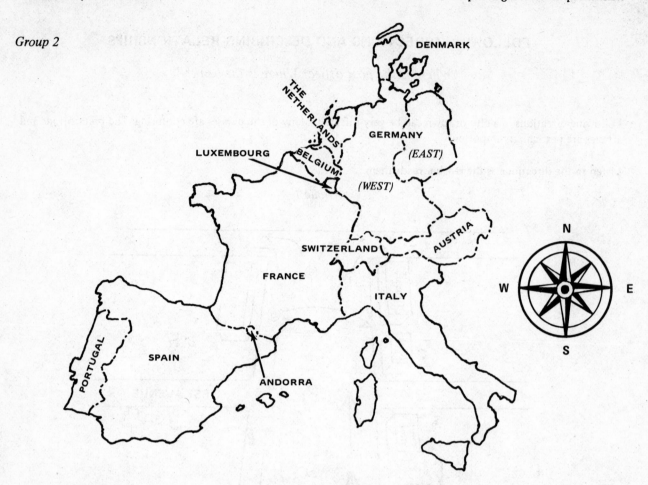

Listen to the questions. Look at the map. Write the answers. Write whole sentences.

1. _____

2. _____

3. _____

4. _____

5. _____

6. _____

7. _____

8. _____

AURAL COMPREHENSION QUESTIONS

1. _____

2. _____

3. _____

4. _____

DISCUSSION TOPICS

1. Discuss and practice these directions orally.

2. Bring in maps or draw diagrams on the blackboard and discuss relationships such as this:

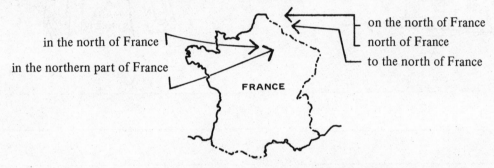

in the north of France

in the northern part of France

on the north of France

north of France

to the north of France

FRANCE

VOCABULARY AND PRONUNCIATION

across the street	around the corner
across the street from	turn the corner
across from	turn at the next corner
straight ahead	on the corner
up the street	onto the curb
straight forward	into the street
forward	next door to
back	the adjoining
down the street	in the middle of the street
straight back	to the north
to the right	on the north
to the left	north of
in the middle of the block	bordered on the east by
on both sides of the street	

DESCRIBING PERSONAL RESIDENCE

"Where do you live? Where is that?"

You can use many different phrases to describe the "place" where you live or the place you are from. Each phrase has a specific preposition which must be used.

Listen carefully. Write the sentence in the correct place. Be sure to write complete sentences.

1.

a. _____

_____

b. _____

_____

2.

a. _____

_____

b. _____

_____

3.

LAKE MICHIGAN

CHICAGO

a. _____

_____

b. _____

_____

4.

FLORIDA

a. _____

_____

b. _____

_____

5.

6.

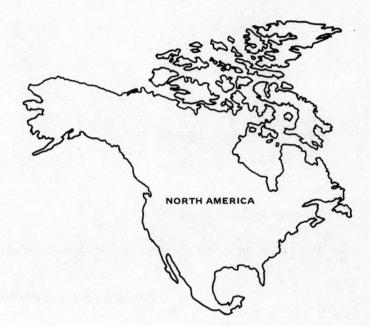

a. _____

_____

b. _____

_____

a. _____

_____

b. _____

_____

AURAL COMPREHENSION QUESTIONS

1. _____

2. _____

3. _____

4. _____

DISCUSSION TOPICS

1. Different ways of describing residence.

2. Make a list of the dozen or more questions which might be asked about the "place" where you live. Discuss.

VOCABULARY AND PRONUNCIATION

at 1632	in the State of Florida
at the dorm	in this county
in room 45	in Lincoln County
on Main Street	in the City and County of Los Angeles
on the street	Chicago is in Cook County.
in Chicago	in Italy
in the city of Chicago	in the U.S.A.
from Chicago	in the country of
from Italy	in North America
in Florida	on the North American continent

LINES, ANGLES, AND SHAPES

"What shape is it? What dimension?"

Here are some useful spatial terms.

Listen carefully. Copy the correct word from the alphabetical list at the right.

Word

1. _____ arc

2. _____ circle

3. _____ concave (lens)

4. _____ cone

5. _____ convex (lens)

6. _____ cube

7. _____ diagonal

8. _____ half circle (semi-circle)

9. _____ horizontal

10. _____ parallel (lines)

11. _____ perpendicular (lines)

12. _____ rectangle

13. _____ right angle

14. _____ sphere

15. _____ square

16. _____ trapezoid

17. _____ triangle

18. _____ vertical

one-dimensional

two-dimensional

three-dimensional

AURAL COMPREHENSION QUESTIONS

1. _____

2. _____

3. _____

4. _____

DISCUSSION TOPIC

1. Dimensions: one-dimensional figures, two-dimensional figures, and three-dimensional figures.

VOCABULARY AND PRONUNCIATION

For pronunciation practice, practice dictating figures for fellow students to draw.

arc	perpendicular
curved line	rectangle
circle	right angle
concave	sphere
cone	square
convex	trapezoid
cube	triangle
diagonal	vertical
half circle	one-dimensional
semi-circle	two-dimensional
horizontal	three-dimensional
parallel	

FILLING OUT CHARTS: PUNCTUATION SIGNS AND SYMBOLS CHART

Each language has punctuation marks which are somewhat different from those in all other languages. English makes use of the following fifteen punctuation marks. Fill out the chart as the teacher dictates.

Listen carefully. First repeat the vocabulary. Then follow the directions as the teacher dictates. Use the symbols in the column at the right. Notice they are alphabetized for your convenience.

Columns

Rows

apostrophe *s*	('s)
cents sign	(¢)
colon	(:)
comma	(,)
dash marks (2 hyphens)	(– –)
dollar sign	($)
et cetera sign	(etc.)
exclamation point (mark)	(!)
parenthesis marks	((. . .))
period	(.)
question mark	(?)
quotation marks	(" . . . ")
semicolon	(;)
slash mark	(/)
star (asterisk)	(*)

AURAL COMPREHENSION QUESTIONS

1. _____

2. _____

3. _____

4. _____

DISCUSSION TOPIC

1. Punctuation marks and their uses.

VOCABULARY AND PRONUNCIATION

apostrophe

cents sign

colon

comma

dash mark

dollar sign

et cetera sign

exclamation point

parenthesis

question mark

quotation marks

semicolon

slash mark

star

asterisk

left-hand column

right-hand column

middle column

_____

top row

bottom row

middle row

_____

2nd from the top

2nd from the bottom

FILLING OUT CHARTS: MATHEMATICAL SIGNS AND SYMBOLS

Mathematical signs and symbols are used in much the same form throughout the world. However, it is important to know the English names for the signs and symbols.

Listen carefully. First repeat the vocabulary words. Then, follow the directions as the teacher dictates. Use the symbols in the column at the right. Notice they are in alphabetical order for your convenience.

Columns

Rows

decimal point two five	(.25)
division sign	(÷)
equal sign	(=)
fifty percent	(50%)
less than	(<)
minus sign	(−)
more than	(>)
multiplication sign	(X)
not equal to	(≠)
number sign	(#)
pi	(π)
plus	(+)
square root	($\sqrt{}$)
sum	(Σ)
three fourths	(¾)

AURAL COMPREHENSION QUESTIONS

1. _____

2. _____

3. _____

4. _____

DISCUSSION TOPIC

1. Mathematical symbols and their uses.

VOCABULARY AND PRONUNCIATION

left hand column	mathematical signs
right hand column	mathematical symbols
middle column	_____
2nd from the left	plus sign
2nd from the right	minus sign
top row	division sign
bottom row	multiplication sign
middle row	_____
_____	one-quarter
decimal point	one-fourth
_____	twenty-five percent
less than	_____
more than	one-half
equal sign	fifty-percent
not equal to	_____
number sign	three-quarters
pi	three-fourths
square root	seventy-five percent
sum	

GEOGRAPHICAL LOCATIONS: THE WESTERN STATES

Extending from the Pacific Ocean east to the Rocky Mountains lie eleven western states. These eleven states are part of the 48 continental states of the United States. In addition there are two more states which border on the Pacific Ocean. One is Hawaii and one is Alaska.

Most of these western states are large in area. Many are sparsely populated. Some of the most beautiful scenery in the country is found in these states. Mining, cattle and sheep, forest products, and grain are major items in the economies of these states.

Listen carefully. Practice the vocabulary aloud. Then locate each state as the teacher describes its location. Put the name in the proper space on the map.

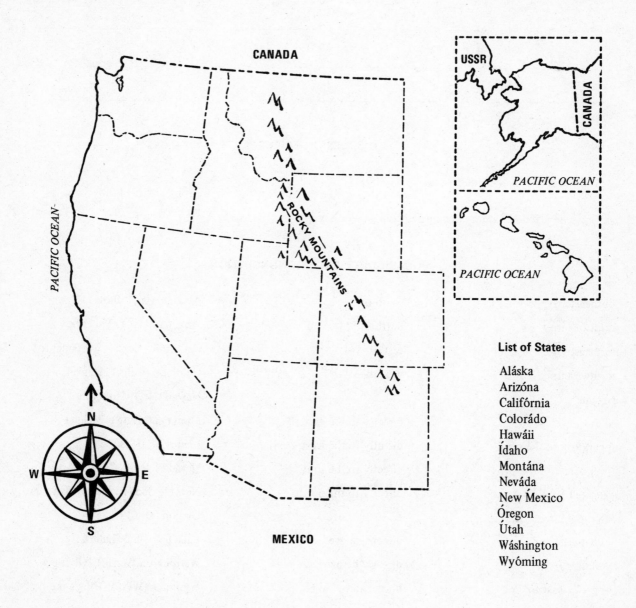

List of States

Aláska
Arizóna
Califórnia
Colorádo
Hawáii
Ídaho
Montána
Neváda
New México
Óregon
Útah
Wáshington
Wyóming

AURAL COMPREHENSION QUESTIONS

1. _____

   _____

2. _____

   _____

3. _____

   _____

4. _____

   _____

DISCUSSION TOPICS

1. The states and their capitals.

2. Geographical description of countries (using a world map).

VOCABULARY AND PRONUNCIATION

southeastern	south of	Alaska (Alas.) - Juneau
southwestern	north of	Arizona (Ariz.) - Phoenix
northeastern	east of	California (Calif.) - Sacramento
northwestern	west of	Colorado (Colo.) - Denver
extreme	_____	Hawaii (Ha.) - Honolulu
far	directly to the east	Montana (Mont.) - Helena
uppermost on the map	directly to the west	Idaho (Ida.) - Boise
lower part	directly to the south	Nevada (Nev.) - Carson City
is located	directly to the north	New Mexico (N. Mex.) - Sante Fe
lies in the _____		Oregon (Ore.) - Salem
lies between	_____	Utah (U.) - Salt Lake City
extending from	directly above	Washington (Wash.) - Olympia
from X east to Y	directly below	Wyoming (Wyo.) - Cheyenne
continental states	borders on	

GEOGRAPHICAL LOCATIONS: THE NORTHEASTERN STATES

This area contains twelve states. It includes the six New England states, three eastern industrial states, and three Great Lakes states. Many are heavily populated states. Many have large metropolitan areas which are referred to by the term "megalopolis."

Listen carefully. Practice the vocabulary aloud. Then locate each state as the teacher describes its location. Put the name in the proper space on the map.

List of States

Connécticut	Massachúsetts	New Jérsey	Pennsylvánia
Indiána	Míchigan	New Yórk	Rhode Ísland
Máine	New Hámpshire	Ohío	Vermónt

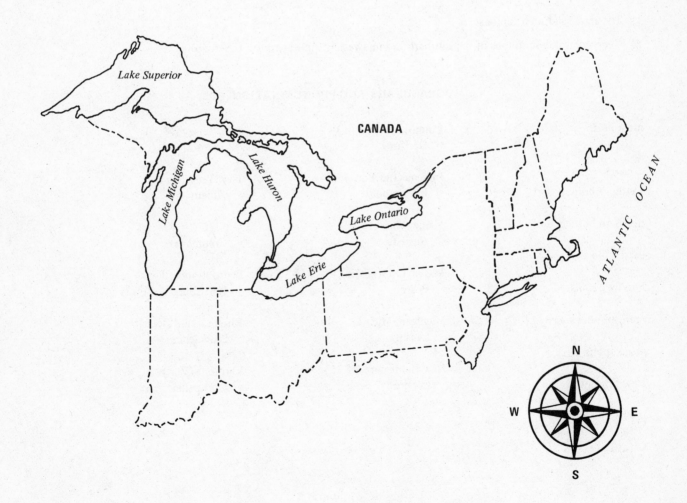

119

AURAL COMPREHENSION QUESTIONS

1. _____

   _____

2. _____

   _____

3. _____

   _____

4. _____

   _____

DISCUSSION TOPICS

1. The states and their capitals.
2. Geographical descriptions of the southern and midwestern states (using a U.S. map).

VOCABULARY AND PRONUNCIATION

most northerly state

in two parts

southern border

northern border

eastern border

heavily populated

metropolitan areas

megalopolis

New England

industrial states

Great Lakes

Connecticut (Conn.)
   Hartford

Indiana (Ind.)
   Indianapolis

Maine (Me.)
   Augusta

Massachusetts (Mass.)
   Boston

Michigan (Mich.)
   Lansing

New Hampshire (N. H.)
   Concord

New Jersey (N. J.)
   Trenton

New York (N. Y.)
   Albany

Ohio (O.)
   Columbus

Pennsylvania (Penn.)
   Harrisburg

Rhode Island (R. I.)
   Providence

Vermont (Ver.)
   Montpelier

120

GRAPHS (1)

The word graph is an abbreviation for "graphic formula." A graph is a chart which shows changes in the value of a quantity or a quality. This graph is a *bar graph*. The *horizontal* axis of the bar graph is called the *abscissa*. The *vertical* axis of the bar graph is called the *ordinate*.

Teachers in many fields of study use graphs. They may ask you to look at certain items. Often these directions will be given verbally. The following data were prepared by the Bureau of the Census, U. S. Department of Commerce.

Fill in the information on these graphs as the teacher dictates. Abbreviate billion as bil.

GOVERNMENT EXPENDITURES

Billions of Dollars

LOCAL
STATE
FEDERAL

Years

AURAL COMPREHENSION QUESTIONS

1. _____

2. _____

3. _____

4. _____

DISCUSSION TOPICS

1. Bar graphs and their uses.

2. Government expenditures.

VOCABULARY AND PRONUNCIATION

abscissa (horizontal axis)

ordinate (vertical axis)

quantity

quality

bar chart

abbreviation

graphic formula

diagram

government expenditures

billions of dollars

local government

state government

federal government

GRAPHS (2)

The two diagrams in this exercise are *pie graphs*. The parts of a pie graph are called sections, parts, or *sectors*. It is important to be able to understand information given in pie graphs. The following percentages were published by the Bureau of the Census, U. S. Department of Commerce.

Fill in the information on these graphs as the teacher dictates.

FEDERAL BUDGET FOR A RECENT YEAR

RECEIPTS: MONEY RECEIVED

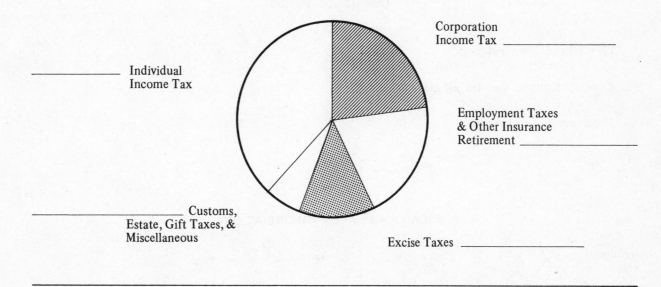

OUTLAYS: MONEY SPENT

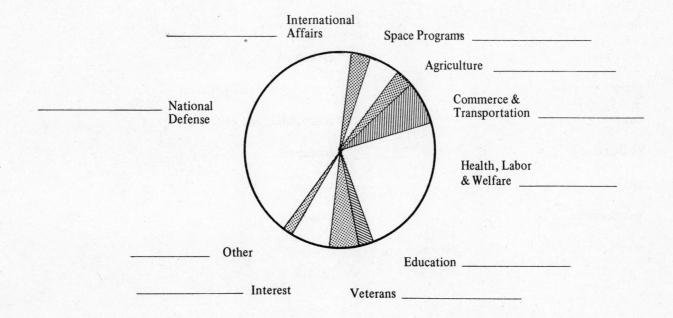

AURAL COMPREHENSION QUESTIONS

1. _____

2. _____

3. _____

4. _____

DISCUSSION TOPICS

1. Pie graphs and their uses.

2. Government money received and spent.

3. Departments of government.

4. Tax sources.

VOCABULARY AND PRONUNCIATION

receipts

individual income tax

corporation income tax

employment tax

insurance

retirement

excise

customs

estate tax

gift tax

miscellaneous

pie graph

sector

outlays

international affairs

national defense

space programs

agriculture

commerce and transportation

health, labor, and welfare

education

veterans

interest

EUROPE

"Where is Lisbon? How far? What direction?"

Describing geographical relationships and distances is done by using compass directions, relative spatial terms, and mileage figures.

Leave the city blank. Write the distances in miles. Write the compass direction. You may abbreviate the compass direction. Follow this example:

[_____ __**215**__ miles __**S S E**__ of London.]

City		Miles	Direction		City		Miles	Direction
1. _____	___ mi.	___	of Paris		9. _____	___ mi.	___	of Oslo
2. _____	___ mi.	___	of Lisbon		10. _____	___ mi.	___	of Stockholm
3. _____	___ mi.	___	of Madrid		11. _____	___ mi.	___	of Helsinki
4. _____	___ mi.	___	of Rome		12. _____	___ mi.	___	of Moscow
5. _____	___ mi.	___	of Bern		13. _____	___ mi.	___	of Warsaw
6. _____	___ mi.	___	of Brussels		14. _____	___ mi.	___	of Budapest
7. _____	___ mi.	___	of Amsterdam		15. _____	___ mi.	___	of Belgrade
8. _____	___ mi.	___	of Copenhagen		16. _____	___ mi.	___	of Sofia

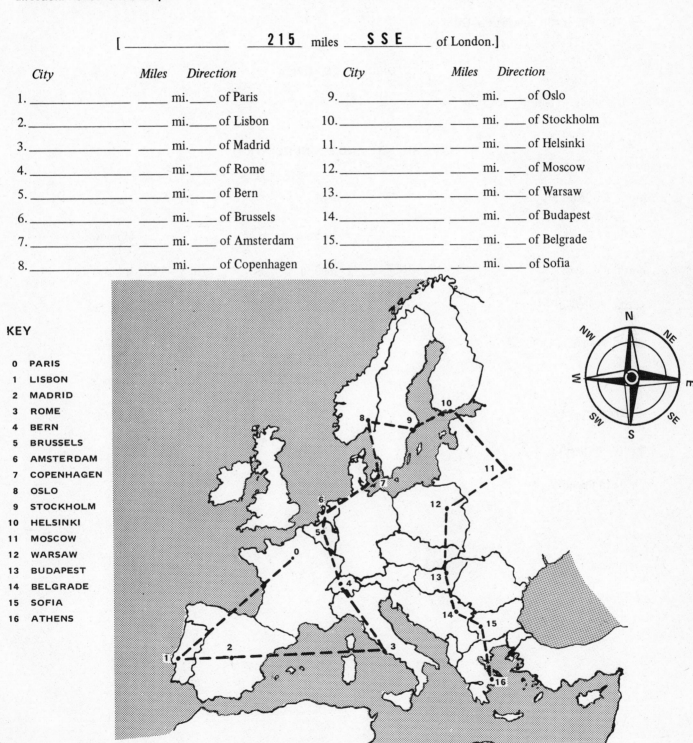

KEY

0 PARIS
1 LISBON
2 MADRID
3 ROME
4 BERN
5 BRUSSELS
6 AMSTERDAM
7 COPENHAGEN
8 OSLO
9 STOCKHOLM
10 HELSINKI
11 MOSCOW
12 WARSAW
13 BUDAPEST
14 BELGRADE
15 SOFIA
16 ATHENS

PROBLEM

Fill in the names of the cities on page 125. (Notice the numbers in the lesson match the numbers on the map.) Then answer these questions.

1. What city is 240 miles almost straight east of Lisbon?

2. What city is 790 miles south, southeast of Helsinki?

3. What city is 445 miles northwest of Rome?

4. What city is 430 miles east of Oslo?

DISCUSSION TOPIC

1. Distances — countries of Europe.

VOCABULARY AND PRONUNCIATION

south, southeast	Paris	Helsinki
south, southwest	Lisbon	Moscow
north, northeast	Madrid	Warsaw
north, northwest	Rome	Budapest
almost straight east of	Bern	Sofia
almost due east of	Brussels	Belgrade
straight south of	Amsterdam	Athens
slightly north of	Copenhagen	London
a little to the north of	Oslo	Stockholm

AIR MILES

"How many miles? Which direction?"

Let us look at some relative distances. We will compare air mileages from New York City to all points of the compass.

Listen carefully.

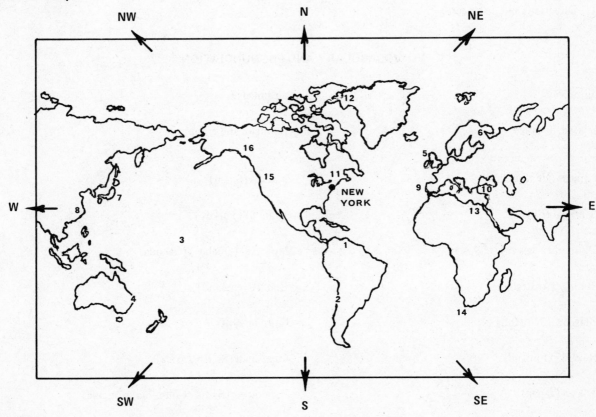

Group # 1	Group # 2	Group # 3	Group # 4
a. _____	e. _____	i. _____	m. _____
b. _____	f. _____	j. _____	n. _____
c. _____	g. _____	k. _____	o. _____
d. _____	h. _____	l. _____	p. _____

Group # 1	Group # 2	Group # 3	Group # 4
1. Caracas	5. Glasgow	9. Madrid	13. Cairo
2. Santiago	6. Helsinki	10. Istanbul	14. Capetown
3. Honolulu	7. Tokyo	11. Montreal	15. Vancouver
4. Sydney	8. Shanghai	12. Greenland (Etah)	16. Juneau

PROBLEM

Within each group (i.e., 1, 2, 3, and 4) match mileage figure and compass direction with the correct city below. Use the map. Ask your teacher for help if necessary.

DISCUSSION TOPIC

1. Directions and distances.

VOCABULARY AND PRONUNCIATION

air miles   air mileage

relative distance   points of the compass

_____   _____

Caracas (Venezuela)   Madrid (Spain)

Santiago (Chile)   Istanbul (Turkey)

Honolulu (Hawaii) (U.S.A.)   Montreal (Quebec) (Canada)

Sydney (Australia)   Etah (Greenland)

Glasgow (Scotland)   Cairo (Egypt)

Helsinki (Finland)   Capetown (South Africa)

Tokyo (Japan)   Vancouver (British Columbia) (Canada)

Shanghai (China)   Juneau (Alaska) (U.S.A.)

SAKS FIFTH AVENUE

"Where are the hats? Where are the shirts?"

In a large department store the elevator operator can tell you where to find merchandise. The Men's Department of Saks' New York store is on the 6th floor. Let us locate some items.

Listen carefully. Practice the vocabulary. Then write the names on the diagram as you hear them.

```
SAKS FIFTH AVENUE — MEN'S DEPARTMENT

  #1              #4                  #9

                                      #10
  #2
             #5       #6

                                    #11

  #3      #7       #8                #12

     Elevator①    Elevator②    Elevator③
```

Ties – Number _____   Shoes – Number _____

Hats – Number _____   Jewelry – Number _____

Bathrobes – Number _____   Suits – Number _____

Pajamas – Number _____   Top Coats – Number _____

Sweaters – Number _____   Sport Jackets – Number _____

Underwear – Number _____   Shirts – Number _____

129

PROBLEM

Look at the bottom of page 129. Put the number of the correct counter beside each item of clothing. Ask your teacher for help if necessary.

DISCUSSION TOPICS

1. Department store arrangement of items.

2. Store directory for locating items in a clothing store.

3. Other clothing items for men, women, and children.

VOCABULARY AND PRONUNCIATION

department store	ties
elevator operator	hats
Men's Department	bathrobes
_____	pajamas
shoes	sweaters
slippers	underwear
jewelry	_____
suits	clear to the back of the store*
top coats	way at the back*
sport jackets	way up front*
shirts	all the way back*

---

*Informal phrases.

SUPER-X GROCERY

"Where is the meat? Where are the frozen foods?"

In large grocery stores the clerks can tell you where to find certain foods. Let us locate some items.

Listen carefully. Practice the vocabulary. Then write the names on the diagram as you hear them.

THE BACK

```
                              #8        #7              #6

        #9        #11 #12    #13 #14      #15 #16     #17 #18      #5

                                      X
                #10      #3      #3      #3      #3
                                 ↗      ↗       ↗       ↗
                              CHECK-OUT STANDS

#1   DOOR          #2  ────────►                    #4
                      BASKETS
```

THE FRONT

Door – Number _____1_____	Canned Fruit – Number _____
Baskets – Number _____2_____	Canned Vegetables – Number _____
Check-out Stands – Number _____3_____	Drugs – Number _____
Dairy Products – Number _____	Frozen Food – Number _____
Meat – Number _____	Soaps and Cleaners (cleaning products) – Number _____
Produce (fresh fruits and vegetables) – Number _____	Paper Products – Number _____
Ice Cream – Number _____	Coffee, Tea, etc. – Number _____
Cookies – Number _____	Soft Drinks – Number _____
Bread – Number _____	Dishes (and utensils) – Number _____

PROBLEM

_____

_____

_____

_____

DISCUSSION TOPICS

1. Grocery store arrangement of foodstuffs.

2. Store directory for locating items in a grocery store.

3. Other grocery items.

VOCABULARY AND PRONUNCIATION

clerks	bread
baskets	produce
check-out stands	(fresh fruits)
food stuffs (i.e., foods)	(fresh vegetables)
_____	canned goods
meat	soaps
dairy products	cleaners
cookies	coffee
soft drinks (i.e., Coke, Pepsi, etc.)	tea
frozen foods	dishes
ice cream	utensils
	drugs

SHOPPING DISTRICT

"Where is the bank? Where is the theater?"

Shopping districts in most small towns have almost identical stores and buildings. Let us locate some of these.

Listen carefully. Practice the vocabulary. Then write the names on the map.

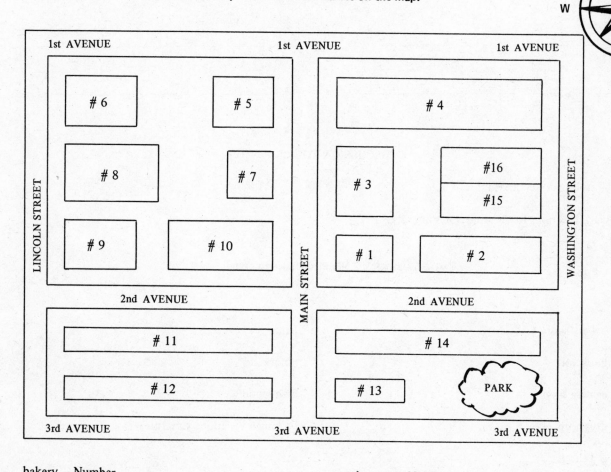

bakery – Number _____

bank – Number _____

bookstore – Number _____

camera shop – Number _____

drug store – Number _____

gift shop – Number _____

Harris High School – Number _____

library – Number _____

men's store – Number _____

parking lot – Number _____

record shop – Number _____

sporting goods – Number _____

theater – Number _____

women's shop – Number _____

YMCA – Number _____

YWCA – Number _____

PROBLEM

_____

_____

_____

_____

DISCUSSION TOPICS

1. The stores and services in this exercise.

2. Giving directions for locating stores in a city.

VOCABULARY AND PRONUNCIATION

Stores	*Services*
bakery shop	bank
bookstore	library
camera shop	high school
drugstore	parking lot (parking structure)
gift shop	theater
record shop	YMCA
sporting goods	YWCA
women's store	

SHOPS AND SERVICES

"Where is the shoe repair? Where is the post office?"

Let us locate some of the usual shops and service buildings.

Listen carefully. Practice the vocabulary. Then write the names on the map as you hear them.

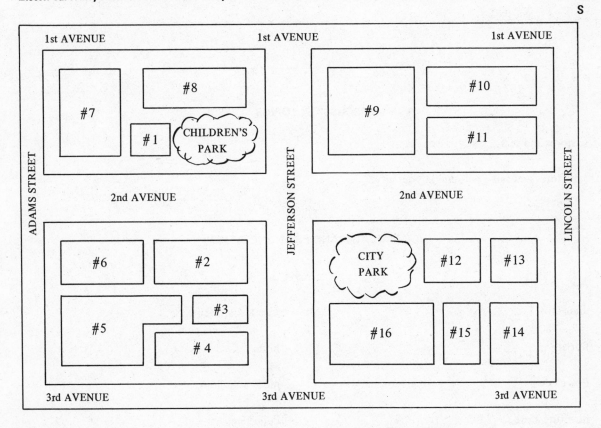

dime store — Number _____

Fire Department — Number _____

flower shop (florist) — Number _____

furniture store — Number _____

grocery store — Number _____

hardware store — Number _____

hotel — Number _____

laundry — Number _____

medical building — Number _____

paint store — Number _____

Police Dept. — Number _____

Post Office — Number _____

restaurant — Number _____

Salvation Army — Number _____

shoe repair shop — Number _____

Western Union — Number _____

PROBLEM

_____

_____

_____

_____

DISCUSSION TOPICS

1. The stores and services in this exercise.

2. Other stores and services found in your city.

VOCABULARY AND PRONUNCIATION

Stores

    dime store*

    florist

    flower shop

    furniture store

    grocery store

    hardware store

    laundry

    paint store

Services

    Fire Department

    hotel

    medical building

    Police Department

    Post Office

    restaurant

    Salvation Army

    shoe repair shop

    Western Union

---

*A variety store such as Kresge, Kress, Woolworth, etc.

SPACE PUZZLE: WHO PLAYS THE GUITAR?

Five students from five different countries were studying English in the United States. They lived in adjoining houses. They planned to study in five different fields of study in five different cities. Each of the five had a different hobby.

Listen carefully. First practice the vocabulary. Then listen to each statement. Find the correct square. Write the correct word from the list below.

	RED HOUSE	BLUE HOUSE	GREEN HOUSE	WHITE HOUSE	PURPLE HOUSE
Country					
Field					
City					
Hobby					

Country	*City*	*Field*	*Hobby*
Turkey	San Francisco	Engineering	dancing
Peru	Miami	Law	soccer
Korea	Chicago	Business	swimming
Spain	New York	Chemistry	travel
India	Boston	Psychology	playing the guitar

TEST

Refer to page 137 and answer these questions.

1. Who plays the guitar?

2. Who is going to study in San Francisco?

3. Who is going to study in the field of Business?

DISCUSSION TOPIC

1. Fields of study — countries — cities — hobbies.

VOCABULARY AND PRONUNCIATION

Turkey	San Francisco
Peru	Miami
Korea	Chicago
Spain	New York
India	Boston
————	————
Engineering	dancing
Law	soccer
Business	swimming
Chemistry	travel
Psychology	playing the guitar

SPACE PUZZLE: WHO IS 18 YEARS OLD?

Six students from six different countries were studying English in the United States. They lived in six adjoining apartments. They planned to study in six different fields of study. They drove six different cars, they enjoyed six different sports, and they were six different ages.

Listen to each statement. Find the correct square. Write the correct word from the list below.

	Apt. #1	Apt. #2	Apt. #3	Apt. #4	Apt. #5	Apt. #6
Country						
Field						
Car						
Sport						
Age						

Country	*Field*	*Car*	*Sport*	*Age*
Greece	Anthropology	Cadillac	baseball	19
Iran	Biology	Mercedes	bicycling	18
Japan	History	Mustang	golf	20
Mexico	Linguistics	Pinto	polo	27
Thailand	Medicine	Volkswagen	swimming	29
Venezuela	Physics	Volvo	tennis	36

TEST

Refer to page 139 and answer these questions:

1. Who is 18 years old?

2. Who drives a Pinto?

3. Who plays tennis?

DISCUSSION TOPIC

1. Fields of study — cars — countries — sports.

VOCABULARY AND PRONUNCIATION

Greece	Anthropology
Iran	Biology
Japan	History
Mexico	Linguistics
Thailand	Medicine
Venezuela	Physics
————	————
Cadillac	baseball
Mercedes	bicycling
Mustang	golf
Pinto	polo
Volkswagen	swimming
Volvo	tennis

VOCABULARY LIST
DIRECTIONS AND SPATIAL RELATIONSHIPS

Write your own list of new words. Please review this list and be sure you know each vocabulary item.

_____

_____

_____

_____

_____

_____

_____

_____

_____

_____

_____

turn the page

VOCABULARY (continued)

_____   _____

_____   _____

_____   _____

_____   _____

_____   _____

_____   _____

_____   _____

_____   _____

_____   _____

_____   _____

_____   _____

_____   _____

_____   _____

Unit 4
Time and Temporal Sequence

Unit 4

Time and Temporal Sequence

Time and temporal concepts in a new language are often confusing. Ideas about time and the phrases used to express these ideas are sometimes difficult to learn. In English there are many alternate ways of expressing a single time "idea." This unit will present some of these. Be sure to ask questions and discuss the unit with your teacher.

The goals of this unit are:

   . . . to provide practice with time and temporal vocabulary

   . . . to present information about time and temporal concepts.

The six *Review Lessons* include defining solar and standard time, telling time, adverbs of frequency, time sequence and temporal order, contrasting points of time with periods of time (i.e., punctual versus durative), and time measurements used as adjectives.

Five *Context Lessons* emphasize time tables, time zones and time changes. Four *Problem Lessons* provide real-life uses of time in public transportation and travel. The two *Test Lessons* present practical word problems.

SOLAR TIME AND STANDARD TIME

The rotation of the earth and the vertical rays of the sun determine time. Time changes four minutes for each degree of longitude or one hour for each fifteen degrees. If each place on the earth used its own solar time, however, it would be confusing. Therefore, the earth has been divided into 24 standard time zones, each one approximately 15 degrees. Additional changes of time have been made in some locations.

Listen carefully. Write the longitude and time as the teacher dictates. Follow New York as an example. Notice that this lesson uses NUMBERS, LETTERS, DIRECTIONS and TIMES.

City	Longitude	Time
Peking		
Melbourne		
Auckland		
Honolulu		
San Francisco		
Mexico City		
New York	73° 58′ W	1:00 pm
São Paulo		
Reykjavik		
Paris		
Moscow		
Calcutta		

AURAL COMPREHENSION QUESTIONS

1. _____

2. _____

3. _____

4. _____

DISCUSSION TOPICS

1. Greenwich Meridian — Greenwich mean time — International Date Line — longitude.

2. Each city and its antipode.*

VOCABULARY AND PRONUNCIATION

solar time

standard time

24 time zones

rotation of the earth

vertical rays of the sun

longitude

degrees

minutes

zero degrees — twenty minutes

thirty degrees East of Greenwich

sixty degrees West of Greenwich

Greenwich Mean Time

Greenwich Meridian

International Dateline

antipode*

farthest point

opposite side of the earth

_____

*Antipode means the exact opposite side of the earth. The place on earth which is farthest away from you now is your antipode.

TIME

60 seconds (sec.) = 1 minute (min.)

60 minutes   = 1 hour (hr.)

24 hours   = 1 day

15 minutes   = a quarter of an hour

30 minutes   = half an hour

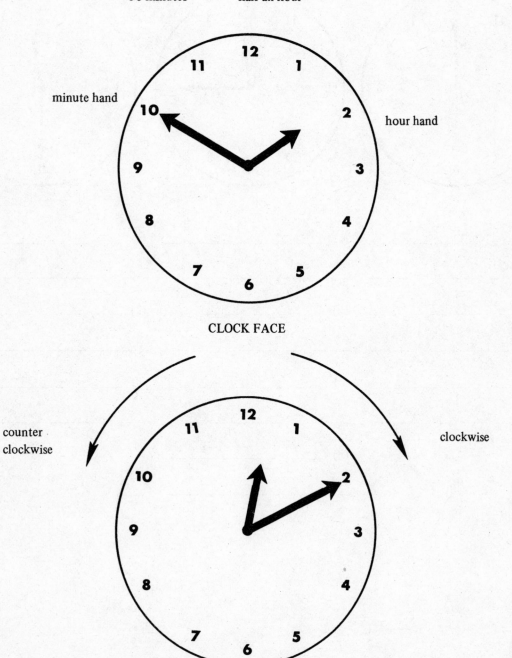

CLOCK FACE

TELLING TIME: TIME PHRASES

"What time is it? Is it a quarter after? Is it ten till?"

There are many different ways to express a given time. We will review a few of the most common expressions.

Listen carefully. Listen to the sentence. Remember the time phrase. Find the correct clock. Write the time phrase under the correct clock. You do not need to write a.m. or p.m. See how fast you can work.

(a) _____   (a) _____   (a) _____

_____   _____   _____

(b) _____   (b) _____   (b) _____

_____   _____   _____

(c) _____   (c) _____   (c) _____

_____   _____   _____

                              (d) _____

                              _____

(a) _____

_____

(b) _____

_____

(c) _____

_____

(d) _____

_____

(a) _____

_____

(b) _____

_____

(c) _____

_____

(d) _____

_____

(a) _____

_____

(b) _____

_____

(c) _____

_____

(d) _____

_____

AURAL COMPREHENSION QUESTIONS

1. _____

2. _____

3. _____

4.   (a) _____

     (b) _____

     (c) _____

DISCUSSION TOPICS

1. Minute hand — hour hand — second hand — clockwise — counterclockwise.

2. Alternative time phrases.

VOCABULARY AND PRONUNCIATION

twelve o'clock

12 midnight

12 m

12 noon

12 n

_____

a quarter after

a quarter past

15 minutes past

12:15

_____

half past

30 minutes past the hour of 12

12:30

ten till

ten of

ten minutes before

ten to

12:50

_____

a quarter till

a quarter of

15 minutes till

12:45

_____

ten after

ten past

ten minutes after

12:10

ACTION: ADVERBS OF FREQUENCY

"How often are they late? Usually? Sometimes? Often?"

These words are adverbs of frequency. They describe the frequency with which an action or an event is repeated. This lesson will review some of the most common frequency words. Some of them are single words and some of them are phrases. Be sure to write the *entire* phrase including the prepositions and articles.

Listen carefully. Write adverbs of frequency in the blank space. Work as fast as you can. Check your spelling. Notice that the list at the bottom of the page is alphabetized.

1. Trains in my country are _____ somewhat late.

2. They are _____ _____ at least a few minutes late.

3. They are _____ over 5 minutes late.

4. _____ ___ _____ _____ they are 10 minutes late.

5. _____ they are more than 15 minutes late.

6. _____ they are 20 minutes late.

7. _____ _____ they are 25 minutes late.

8. _____ ___ _____ _____ they are nearly an hour late.

9. _____ they are as much as 45 minutes late.

10. _____ they are 50 minutes late.

11. _____ _____ ___ _____ they are more than an hour late.

12. They have _____ been more than 2 hours late.

13. They are _____ as much as 3 hours late.

14. They are _____ _____ more than 4 hours late.

15. They have _____ been as much as 10 hours late.

almost always	hardly ever	occasionally	seldom
always	many times	often	sometimes
frequently	most of the time	once in a while	usually
half of the time	never	rarely	

100%

50%

0%

AURAL COMPREHENSION QUESTIONS

1. _____

2. _____

3. _____

4. _____

DISCUSSION TOPIC

1. Relative meanings of the frequency words (i.e., order of frequency).

VOCABULARY AND PRONUNCIATION

somewhat late	at least (an hour late)
a little late	over (two hours late)
a few minutes late	more than (four hours late)
five minutes late	as much as (two hours late)
on time	nearly (an hour late)
early	(all frequency adverbs used in this lesson)
late	

TEMPORAL ORDER: SEQUENCE OF EVENTS

*"He left **before** I came. He came **after** I left. He came **while** I was there."*

The first two sentences tell the *order* in which the events occurred. The third sentence gives two events which occurred *at the same time.* There are many phrases used to describe these time relationships.

Listen carefully. Write the missing words. Notice the prepositions are *very* important.

1. He came _____ she left.

2. She left _____ he came.

3. She _____ _____ to class.

4. She arrived _____ the class _____ .

5. He arrived _____ .

6. He got there _____ the appointed time.

7. He studied _____ the bell rang.

8. He _____ to study _____ _____ the bell had rung.

9. He _____ studying _____ the bell had rung.

10. He went swimming _____ class.

11. He went to class _____ he had been swimming.

12. He went swimming _____ he went to class.
    He went to class _____ .

13. He telephoned _____ I was studying.

14. He telephoned _____ _____ _____ I was studying.

15. She read the paper _____ he got breakfast.

16. _____ he was getting breakfast, she was reading the paper.

17. _____ he prepared breakfast, she read the paper.

18. _____ _____ _____ _____ she was reading, he was cooking.

19. The classroom door was locked _____ I arrived.

20. Someone locked the classroom door _____ I arrived.

AURAL COMPREHENSION QUESTIONS

1. _____

2. _____

3. _____

4. _____

DISCUSSION TOPIC

1. Temporal order.

VOCABULARY AND PRONUNCIATION

temporal order	at the same time
sequence	while
sequential	during
early	during the same time
late	at the same time as
before	as
after	It was over *when* I arrived.
afterwards	appointed hour
continued to	got breakfast
even though	to get breakfast = to prepare breakfast
although	

DESCRIBING TIME: PUNCTUAL VERSUS DURATIVE

"He left **at three o'clock.** *He worked* **for two hours."**

The first sentence tells an exact (or punctual) *point* in time. The second gives a *length* of time (duration of time).
There are many phrases used to describe these time relationships.

Listen carefully. Write the missing words. Notice the prepositions are very important.

POINTS OF TIME (PUNCTUAL)

1. He left _____ _____ _____ .

2. He left _____ ____ _____ . .

3. She arrived _____ _____ .

4. She came _____ _____ .

5. She came _____ approximately _____ .

6. He arrived ____ _____ .

7. He arrived punctually ____ ___ _____ _____ .

PERIODS OF TIME (DURATION)

8. He worked _____ _____ _____ _____ .

9. He worked _____ _____ _____ .

10. He worked _____ _____ .

11. He studied _____ ____ _____ .

12. He studied _____ _____ ___ ____ _____ .

13. He worked _____ _____ _____ _____ _____ _____ .

14. He worked _____ _____ _____ ____ _____ _____ .

15. He worked _____ _____ _____ .   8:00 ———→ 5:00

16. It _____ at 8:00 and _____ at 10:00.

17. It _____ at 8:00 and _____ _____ ___ _____ .

155

AURAL COMPREHENSION QUESTIONS

1. _____

2. _____

3. _____

4. _____

DISCUSSION TOPICS

1. Point of time:

        at   at

        C **X** _____   _____ **X** D

2. Duration of time:

        from   to

        A - - - - - - - - - - - ▶ B

3. Termination point:

        _____ until | E

4. Temporal versus spatial (i.e., time versus space).

VOCABULARY AND PRONUNCIATION

duration of time

    from 9:00 until 5:00

    beginning at 6:00

    and ending at 8:00

    starting at 4:00

    finished by 9:00

    completed by 10:00

    a 3-hour time period

    a period of 3½ hours

    all morning

    for two hours

    during the hours of 8 to 5

    between the hours of 6 and 8

exact point of time

    at 6:00

    at 5:00 sharp

    right at 2:00

    about 4:00

    around 9:00

    at approximately 3:00

    on time

    at the appointed time

MEASURING TIME: TIME PERIODS USED AS ADJECTIVES

"How long was your trip? It was a 3-week trip."
"How long does the B.A. degree take? It's a 4-year degree."

We often use time adjectives of this kind to describe periods of time. Notice a hyphen is used and the singular *not* the plural form is used.

Listen carefully. Write down the time adjective. They will be given in order.

Example: a 3-hour wait

second

_____ delay

_____ countdown

day

_____ week

_____ wait

year

_____ contract

_____ degree

minute

_____ movie

_____ test

week

_____ vacation

_____ cruise

decade

_____ treaty

_____ agreement

hour

_____ course

_____ flight

month

_____ baby

_____ girl

century

_____ period of time

_____ span of time

a ten-year-old boy

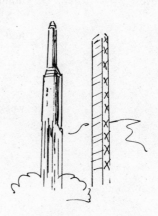

a 90-second countdown

AURAL COMPREHENSION QUESTIONS

1. _____

2. _____

3. _____

4. _____

DISCUSSION TOPICS

1. Ways to use time adjectives.

2. Additional time adjectives — add to this list.

>   a 45-second race
>
>   a 15-minute speech
>
>   a 3-week trip
>
>   a 75-year-old man

VOCABULARY AND PRONUNCIATION

time periods	second	month
used as adjectives	minute	year
singular form	hour	decade
hyphen	day	century
	week	

TIME TABLES: GREYHOUND BUS SCHEDULE

"When does the next bus from Chicago arrive? What time do buses leave for Detroit?"

Sometimes it is necessary to call a bus station to ask about times of arrivals and departures. This lesson is for instant recognition of time.

Listen carefully. Write the times as the teacher dictates them. Work as fast as you can.

GREYHOUND BUS SCHEDULE
(Ft. Wayne, Indiana)

ARRIVALS FROM			*DEPARTURES TO*	
_____ _____	Chicago	_____ _____
_____ _____	Toledo	_____ _____
_____ _____	Detroit	_____
_____ _____	Cleveland	_____ _____
_____	Indianapolis	_____

AURAL COMPREHENSION QUESTIONS

1. _____

2. _____

3. _____

4. _____

DISCUSSION TOPIC

1. Bus schedules — train schedules.

VOCABULARY AND PRONUNCIATION

Greyhound Bus Company	bus from Chicago	Chicago (Illinois)
bus schedule	leave	Detroit (Michigan)
time table	depart	Indianapolis (Indiana)
arrive	departures	Cleveland (Ohio)
arrivals	bus to Chicago	Toledo (Ohio)

A TOURIST IN NEW YORK CITY: OPENING AND CLOSING HOURS

"What time does it open? When does it close? What time does it begin?"

It is important to know opening and closing hours when visiting a city. Suppose we were going to visit New York City for the first time. Here are some places we might like to visit.

Listen carefully. Write down the correct items.

1. Macy's Department Store

   Tuesdays _____

   Thursdays and Saturdays _____

   Mondays, Wednesdays and Fridays _____

2. Metropolitan Museum of Art

   Mondays — Fridays _____

   Weekends and Holidays _____

3. New York City Ballet
   Evening Performances: Matinee Performances:

   Tuesdays — Saturdays _____   Saturdays _____

   Sundays _____   Sundays _____

4. New York Historical Society

   Daily _____

5. American Stock Exchange (Gallery open)

   Mondays — Fridays _____

6. Empire State Building

   Daily _____

7. Statue of Liberty

   Daily _____

8. United Nations (Guided Tours)

   Daily _____

9. Rockefeller Center

   April 1 — October 1   Daily _____

   October 2 — March 31   Daily _____

10. NBC (Radio and TV Studios)

   Daily _____

SUGGESTION: After this lesson you may wish to begin work on Unit Five (page 183) and alternate lessons from Units Four and Five.

AURAL COMPREHENSION QUESTIONS

1. _____

2. _____

3. _____

4. _____

DISCUSSION TOPIC

1. Usual opening-closing hours of stores and public buildings in your town or campus.

VOCABULARY AND PRONUNCIATION

open daily	from 10 till 2	closes at 5
between the hours of 9 and 12	Mondays through Fridays	begins at 7:30
from 9 to 5	opens at 8	visiting hours
from 8 until 6		closed weekends

NBC	The New York City Ballet	Statue of Liberty
Macy's Department Store	The New York Historical Society	United Nations
The Metropolitan Museum of Art	American Stock Exchange	Rockefeller Center
	Empire State Building	

evening performance	guided tours	gallery
matinee		TV studio

WORLD TIME: TRANSLATING PHRASES

"What time is it in London if it is 5:00 p.m. in Paris?"
"What is the time difference between San Francisco and Tokyo? Is it earlier or later?"

Today rapid communication makes us aware of events throughout the world. Often it is necessary to know the time changes between two places.

Listen carefully. Write the time on the *face* of the correct clock. Always write the time in *numbers* even though different *words* will be used to tell the time. The purpose of this lesson is to give practice in translating time words into time numbers.

Group 1

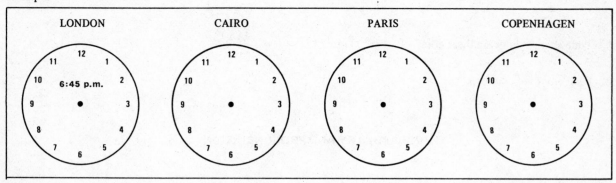

Group 2

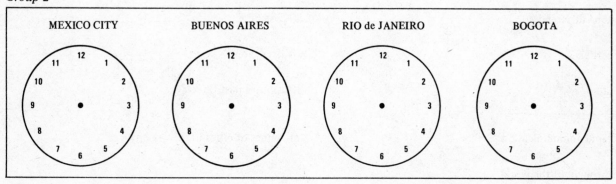

Group 3

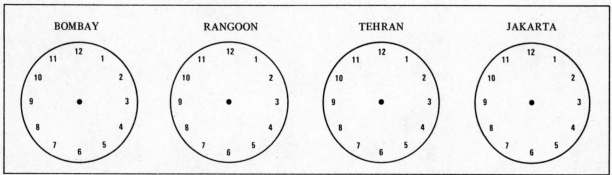

AURAL COMPREHENSION QUESTIONS

1. _____

2. _____

3. _____

4. _____

DISCUSSION TOPICS

1. Time changes between these cities. Earlier? Later?

2. Each city (and country).

VOCABULARY AND PRONUNCIATION

time changes   3:20

time differences   20 past three

earlier   20 after three

later   20 minutes past three
_____

rapid communication   (all names of cities in this lesson)

throughout the world

WORLD TIME: CALCULATING CORRESPONDENCES

"What time is it in Calcutta? How many hours later is it in London?"

With worldwide news coverage today it is important to be able to calculate time correspondences between places.

Listen carefully. Write the time in *numbers* on the face of the correct clock. Often you will have to calculate the time: if the time is *later*, add; if the time is *earlier*. subtract.

> **Example:** It is 1:30 p.m. in New York. Chicago is one hour *earlier.* Therefore, in Chicago it is 12:30 p.m.
> It is 8:15 a.m. in Los Angeles. New York is 3 hours *later.* Therefore, in New York it is 11:15 a.m.

Group 1

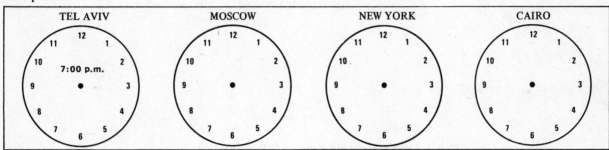

Group 2

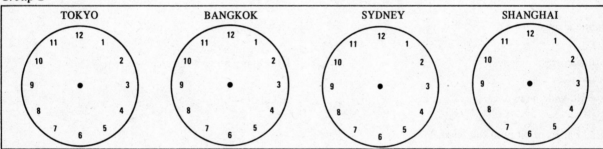

Group 3

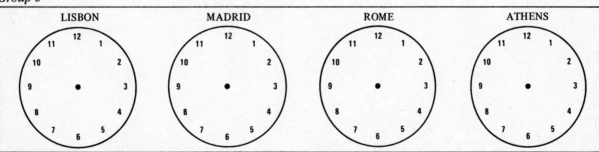

Group 4

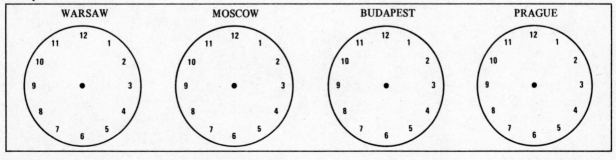

AURAL COMPREHENSION QUESTIONS

1. _____

2. _____

3. _____

4. _____

DISCUSSION TOPICS

1. Calculating time change.

2. Each city (and country).

VOCABULARY AND PRONUNCIATION

time change

time correspondences

world-wide news coverage

(all names of cities in this lesson)

How many hours difference?

How many hours time change?

calculate

STANDARD TIME ZONES OF THE UNITED STATES

"What is the time change between New York and San Francisco? Between Denver and Dallas?"
"What's the difference between Standard Time and Daylight Saving Time?"

The United States is divided into four time zones — Pacific, Mountain, Central and Eastern. There is a three-hour time difference between Pacific Time and Eastern Time. Half the year the country is on Standard Time. The other half of the year — April through October — most of the country is on Daylight Saving Time or "fast time." In most states clocks are set ahead one hour on the last Sunday in April to take advantage of the extra hours of daylight.

Listen carefully. Write the name of the city and the time given.

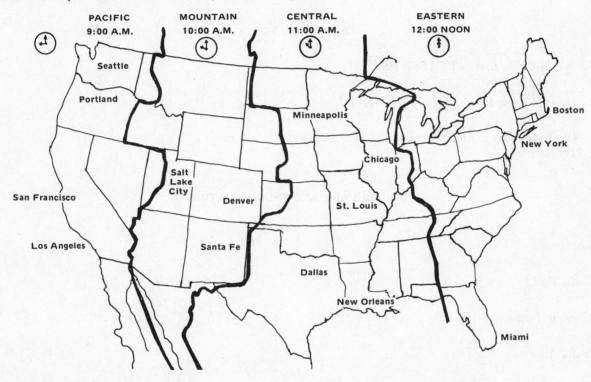

When it is _____ in _____ what time is it in:

City	Time		City	Time
1. _____	_____	8. _____	_____
2. _____	_____	9. _____	_____
3. _____	_____	10. _____	_____
4. _____	_____	11. _____	_____
5. _____	_____	12. _____	_____
6. _____	_____	13. _____	_____
7. _____	_____	14. _____	_____

AURAL COMPREHENSION QUESTIONS

1. _____

2. _____

3. _____

4. _____

DISCUSSION TOPICS

1. Standard time zones — EST; CST; MST; PST.

2. Daylight saving time — EDT; CDT; MDT; PDT.

   (the last Sunday in April to the last Sunday in October).

VOCABULARY AND PRONUNCIATION

time zones

Pacific Time

Mountain Time

Central Time

Eastern Time

Standard Time

Daylight Saving Time

AROUND THE WORLD

Each year students from all over the world study in the United States. Some study only English and return to their homes in a short time. Others study in the fields of science, engineering, law, business administration, medicine, dentistry, linguistics, etc.

In traveling to the United States and then in returning to their homes many students have an opportunity to go around the world. Many of us dream of circling the globe but these lucky students make this dream come true.

Listen carefully. Write the miles and the hours and the minutes.

Maria left Mexico City on August 15. She flew first

	Miles		*Hours and Minutes*
from Mexico City to Rio	_____	in _____	_____
from Rio to Sydney	_____	in _____	_____
from Sydney to Shanghai	_____	in _____	_____
from Shanghai to Bombay	_____	in _____	_____
from Bombay to Baghdad	_____	in _____	_____
from Baghdad to Istanbul	_____	in _____	_____
from Istanbul to Berlin	_____	in _____	_____
from Berlin to New York	_____	in _____	_____
from New York to Mexico City	_____	in _____	_____

PROBLEM

Answer the following questions: (Refer to the information you have written on page 169.)

How many miles did Maria travel?

How many hours was she in the air?

DISCUSSION TOPIC

1. Air speed between cities.

VOCABULARY AND PRONUNCIATION

science	Mexico City
engineering	Rio de Janeiro
law	Sydney
business administration	Shanghai
medicine	Bombay
dentistry	Baghdad
linguistics	Istanbul
opportunity	Berlin
circle the globe	New York

FLIGHT TO SOUTH AMERICA

A Venezuelan student called the airport in San Francisco. He requested information about a flight to Caracas. This is the flight information he received.

Listen carefully. Write the information. Then solve the problem.

City	*AR Time*	*LV Time*
	X X X	
		X X X

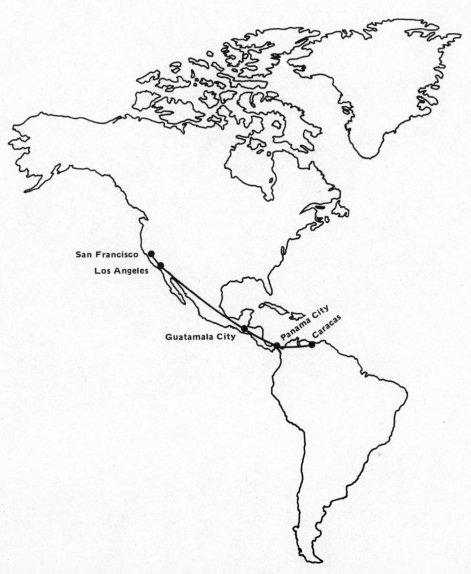

PROBLEM

What was the *actual* number of hours on the trip from San Francisco to Caracas?

Remember, because San Francisco is four hours earlier than Caracas, there is a four-hour time difference. You lose four hours. Therefore you must subtract four hours for the actual total number of hours in the trip.

DISCUSSION TOPIC

1. Hours from Greenwich Mean Time.

VOCABULARY AND PRONUNCIATION

Greenwich Mean Time

Venezuela

Venezuelan

Caracas

San Francisco

Los Angeles

Guatemala City

Panama City

FLIGHT TO THE MIDDLE EAST

A student from Iran called the airport in New York City. He requested information about a flight to Tehran. This is the flight information he received.

Listen carefully. Write the information. Then solve the problem.

City	*AR Time*	*LV Time*
	X X X	
		X X X

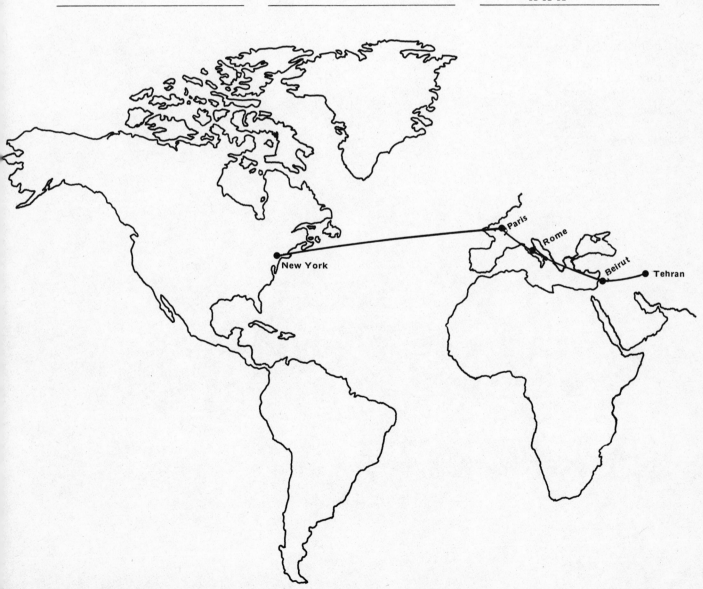

PROBLEM

What was the *actual* number of hours on the trip from New York to Tehran?

Remember, because Tehran is 8½ hours later than New York, there is an 8½-hour time difference. You lose eight and a half hours. You must subtract 8½ hours for the actual total number of hours in the trip.

DISCUSSION TOPIC

1. Reading airline schedules.

VOCABULARY AND PRONUNCIATION

flight information

Middle East

Tehran

Beirut

Paris

Rome

New York

TIME AND LOGIC PUZZLE

Four trains started from four different cities. They reached four other cities at different times. Let us investigate.

Listen carefully. Listen to each statement. Find the correct square. Write the correct word from the list below.

	BLUE TRAIN	RED TRAIN	WHITE TRAIN	GREEN TRAIN
STARTING PLACE				
STARTING TIME				
OCCUPANCY				
SPEED				
ARRIVAL PLACE				
ARRIVAL TIME				

Cities	*Occupancy*	*Speed*	*Arrival Time*	*Starting Time*
New York	200	50 mph	4:00 a.m.	9:00 a.m.
Boston	250	90 mph	3:00 p.m.	11:00 a.m.
Miami	270	100 mph	7:00 a.m.	1:00 a.m.
Chicago	300	300 mph	8:00 p.m.	4:00 p.m.
San Francisco				
Los Angeles				
Philadelphia				

PROBLEM

Please answer the following questions:

1. How many hours in the trip from Boston to Philadelphia?

2. How many hours in the trip from Los Angeles to San Francisco?

3. How many hours in the trip from New York to Miami?

4. How many hours in the trip from Chicago to New York?
   (Remember that Chicago is in the Central time zone and New York and Philadelphia are on Eastern time.)

DISCUSSION TOPIC

1. Time zones — cross country travel.

VOCABULARY AND PRONUNCIATION

New York

Boston

Miami

Chicago

San Francisco

Los Angeles

Philadelphia

investigate

occupancy

PRACTICAL PROBLEMS WITH TIME (1)

"How long?   How often?   What order?" Here are some time problems.

Write the information.

1. _____   4. _____

_____   _____

_____   _____

_____   _____

2. _____   5. _____

_____   _____

_____   _____

3. _____   6. _____

_____   _____

_____   _____

turn the page for #7

7. _____

   _____

   _____

   _____

9. _____

   _____

   _____

   _____

8. _____

   _____

   _____

10. _____

   _____

   _____

TEST

Do the problems. Check your answers with your teacher.

PRACTICAL PROBLEMS WITH TIME (2)

"How long?   How often?   What order?" Here are some more time problems.

Write the information.

1. _____   4. _____

_____   _____

_____   _____

_____   _____

2. _____   5. _____

_____   _____

_____   _____

_____   _____

3. _____   6. _____

_____   _____

_____   _____

_____   _____

turn the page for #7

7. _____   9. _____

_____   _____

_____   _____

_____   _____

8. _____   10. _____

_____   _____

_____   _____

_____   _____

TEST

Do the problems. Check your answers with your teacher.

VOCABULARY LIST
TIME/TEMPORAL RELATIONSHIPS

Write your personal list of new words. Review this list and be sure you know each vocabulary item.

_____   _____

_____   _____

_____   _____

_____   _____

_____   _____

_____   _____

_____   _____

_____   _____

_____   _____

_____   _____

_____   _____

_____   _____

turn the page

VOCABULARY (continued)

_____   _____

_____   _____

_____   _____

_____   _____

_____   _____

_____   _____

_____   _____

_____   _____

_____   _____

_____   _____

_____   _____

_____   _____

_____   _____

Unit 5
Dates and Chronological Order

Unit 5

Dates and Chronological Order

Unit 4 emphasized short periods of time. Unit 5 emphasizes longer periods of time. Be sure to ask questions and discuss this unit with your teacher.

The six *Review Lessons* include relationships between days and weeks and months and years, adverbs of frequency, phrases used to indicate chronological order, and phrases used to indicate reverse chronological order. Six *Context Lessons* provide practice with dates and chronology in the contexts of important explorations, discoveries, population migrations, holidays, and national independence days. Six *Problem Lessons* include history of the English language, memorable events in history, famous men of the past two centuries, world conflicts and struggles, and a chronology of population growth. Two *Test Lessons* complete Unit 5. Both present practical problems.

THE WESTERN CALENDAR

All ancient calendars were lunar calendars. They were based on the time from one full moon to the next. In contrast, the Western calendar used today in many countries is a solar calendar. It is based on the time required for the earth to make one complete revolution around the sun. A solar year is 365 days, five hours, 48 minutes, and 46 seconds. In order to adjust for the extra hours we add one day to the month of February every fourth year and call it leap year.

The calendar is called Western because its use spread through the western part of Europe after the beginning of the Christian era. Remember, the letters B.C. refer to dates before the birth of Christ, while the letters A.D. refer to dates after the birth of Christ.

Listen carefully. Write as the teacher dictates.

Writing Months of the Year

Month   *Abbreviation*

1. _____   _____

2. _____   _____

3. _____   _____

4. _____   _____

5. _____   _____

6. _____   _____

7. _____   _____

8. _____   _____

9. _____   _____

10. _____   _____

11. _____   _____

12. _____   _____

(Check your spelling!!)

January	April	July	October
February	May	August	November
March	June	September	December

Writing Days of the Week

1. _____ (_____)

2. _____ (_____)

3. _____ (_____)

4. _____ (_____)

5. _____ (_____)

6. _____ (_____)

7. _____ (_____)

Years	*Centuries (100 years)*
1. _____	1. _____
2. _____	2. _____
3. _____	3. _____

Decades (10 years)	*Writing Dates*
1. _____	1. *May 4, 1971* _____ *
2. _____	2. _____
3. _____	3. _____

Sunday	Wednesday	Saturday
Monday	Thursday	
Tuesday	Friday	

*Notice, we *write* the date as May 4, 1971, but we often *read* the date with the ordinal form *4th* used for the day of the month.

AURAL COMPREHENSION QUESTIONS

1. _____

2. _____

3. _____

4. _____

DISCUSSION TOPICS

1. Lunar calendars — solar calendars.

2. B.C. and A.D.

3. Capitalization and spelling.

4. Correct written forms for dates.

5. Correct abbreviations.

VOCABULARY AND PRONUNCIATION

western calendar	January (Jan.)	Sunday (Sun.)
ancient	February (Feb.)	Monday (Mon.)
lunar	March (Mar.)	Tuesday (Tues.)
full moon	April (Apr.)	Wednesday (Wed.)
solar	May	Thursday (Thurs.)
one complete revolution	June	Friday (Fri.)
adjust	July	Saturday (Sat.)
leap year	August (Aug.)	in the 1970's
decade	September (Sept.)	in the 1880's
century	October (Oct.)	in the '70's
turn of the century	November (Nov.)	
19th Century	December (Dec.)	

MEASURES OF TIME

60 seconds (sec.)	=	1 minute (min.)
60 minutes (min.)	=	1 hour (hr.)
24 hours	=	1 day
7 days	=	1 week (wk.)
12 months (mo.)	=	1 regular year (yr.)
365 days	=	1 regular year
366 days	=	1 leap year
10 years	=	1 decade
100 years	=	1 century
20 years	=	1 score
2 weeks	=	1 fortnight

In business transactions usually 30 days are considered as one month and 360 days as one year.

Leap years are the centennial years which are divisible by 400 and all other years divisible by four.

A calendar year is from January 1 to December 31. A fiscal year is from July 1 to June 30.

An academic (or school) year is from early September to mid-June.

RELATIONSHIPS BETWEEN DAYS AND WEEKS

"When? What day? What week?"

Many different phrases are used to describe specific days and weeks. We will review a few of the most common expressions.

Listen carefully. Listen to the phrase. Find the correct calendar. Write the phrase.

Group 1

S	M	T	W	Th	F	S
		16				

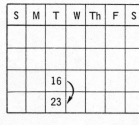

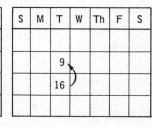

1. _____   2. _____   3. _____

Group 2

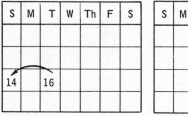

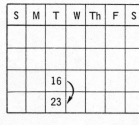

1. _____   2. _____   3. _____   4. _____

_____   _____   _____   _____

Group 3

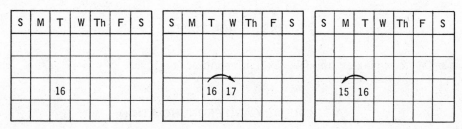

1. _____   2. _____   3. _____

Group 4

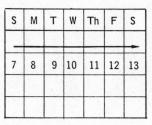

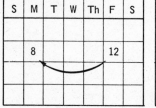

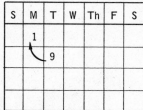

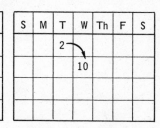

1. _____   2. _____   3. _____   4. _____

_____   _____   _____   _____

AURAL COMPREHENSION QUESTIONS

1. _____

2. _____

3. _____

4. _____

DISCUSSION TOPIC

1. Confusions among these phrases: this fall, next fall, and this coming* fall.

VOCABULARY AND PRONUNCIATION

today	a week from Friday
tomorrow	last Monday
yesterday	this week
the day before yesterday	last week
the day after tomorrow	next week
a week from today	a fortnight = 2 weeks
a week ago	this Friday
a week ago yesterday	next Friday
a week from tomorrow	this coming Friday

_____

*The use of "this coming _____ " is confusing. We insert "coming" whenever the listener might be confused between *this* (day), (week), (month), (season), or (year) and the *next* one. There is a great lack of uniformity among American English speakers. Sometimes it is necessary to ask about the specific *date* or *dates* in order to avoid confusion.

RELATIONSHIPS BETWEEN MONTHS AND YEARS

"When? What month? What year?"

Many different phrases are used to describe specific months and years. We will review a few of the most common expressions.

Listen carefully. Listen to the phrase. Write the correct month. Write the name of the month on the line.

MONTHS

January	February	March	April
May	June	~~July~~	August
September	October	November	December / January

1. _____

2. _____

3. _____

4. _____

5. _____

6. _____

7. _____

YEARS

1969	1970	1971	1972
1973	1974	~~1975~~	1976
1977	1978	1979	1980 / 1981

1. _____

2. _____

3. _____

4. _____

5. _____

6. _____

7. _____

AURAL COMPREHENSION QUESTIONS

1. _____

2. _____

3. _____

4. _____

DISCUSSION TOPIC

1. Confusions among some of the phrases of this lesson.

VOCABULARY AND PRONUNCIATION

this month   this year

next month   next year

month after next   last year

last month   2 years from now

month before last   2 years ago

2 months ago   6 years from now

2 months from now   6 years ago

6 months ago

6 months from now

FREQUENCY ADVERBS: PUBLICATIONS

"How often? Weekly? Biannually? Daily?"

These words describe the frequency with which an action or an event is repeated. This lesson will review some of the most common frequency expressions. Some of them are single words and some of them are phrases.

Listen carefully. Remember the frequency word or phrase. Copy the *number* from the alphabetical list below.

Publication	Frequency (number only)	Publication	Frequency (number only)
Life	_____	*TV Guide*	_____
New York Times	_____	*Time*	_____
National Geographic	_____	*Semester report*	_____
a high school annual	_____	*Quarterly Journal of Speech*	_____
Industrial Stock Index	_____	*Ecology Abstracts*	_____
Reader's Digest	_____	*Playboy*	_____
U.S. Centennial Report	_____	*Psychology Today*	_____
U.S. Government Printing Office Publication List	_____	*U.S. News and World Report*	_____
IBM Stock Report	_____	*Senate Budget Report*	_____
World Almanac	_____	*Garden News*	_____

1. annually
   once a year
   yearly

2. biannually
   twice a year
   semi-annually

3. biennially
   once every two years

4. bimonthly
   once every two months

5. biweekly
   once every two weeks

6. centennially
   once in a hundred years

7. daily
   once a day

8. monthly
   once a month

9. quarterly
   four times a year

10. semiweekly
    twice a week

11. semimonthly
    twice a month

12. weekly
    once a week

AURAL COMPREHENSION QUESTIONS

1. _____

2. _____

3. _____

4. _____

DISCUSSION TOPICS

1. Confusion between biannual and biennial.

2. Confusion in the use of bimonthly and biweekly. (They are sometimes used to mean semimonthly and semi-weekly.)

3. Other publications.

VOCABULARY AND PRONUNCIATION

once in a hundred years

centennially

once in 200 hundred years

bicentennially

once every 50 years

(all frequency words and phrases in this lesson)

semicentennially

once every 150 years

sesquicentennially

once every 300 years

tricentennially

(all publications in this lesson)

CHRONOLOGICAL ORDER: TERRITORIAL EXPANSION

"What order? What sequence?"

Certain words express chronological order. It is important to recognize these words immediately as signals of chronological relationships.

Listen carefully. Write the words of chronological order and the dates.

1. _____ we began with the original 13 states	___ _____ .	819,224 sq. mi.	
2. _____ the Louisiana Purchase was made	___ _____ .	827,192 sq. mi.	
3. _____ Great Britain ceded some land	___ _____ .	69,461 sq. mi.	
4. _____ Florida was acquired	___ _____ .	72,003 sq. mi.	
5. _____ _____ , Texas was added	___ _____ .	390,144 sq. mi.	
6. _____ ____ came the Oregon Territory	___ _____ .	285,580 sq. mi.	
7. _____ ___ ___ was the Mexican Cession	___ _____ .	529,017 sq. mi.	
8. _____ we made the Gadsden Purchase	___ _____ .	29,640 sq. mi.	
9. _____ _____ came the Alaska addition	___ _____ .	586,412 sq. mi.	
10. _____ Hawaii was added	___ _____ .	6,450 sq. mi.	

TOTAL SQUARE MILES   3,615,123 sq. mi.

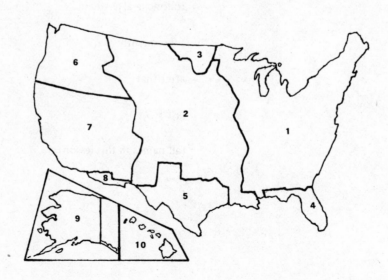

AURAL COMPREHENSION QUESTIONS

1. _____

2. _____

3. _____

4. _____

DISCUSSION TOPICS

1. Chronological order.

2. Territorial expansion.

VOCABULARY AND PRONUNCIATION

order	first
sequence	second
chronological order	then
territory	next
expansion	following that
territorial expansion	immediately after
cede	following after that
ceded	subsequently
cession	after that
was acquired	last
was added	(all names in this lesson)

REVERSE CHRONOLOGY: ANCIENT EMPIRES

"What preceded it? What pre-dated it?"

This lesson will review phrases which indicate reverse chronological order. It also gives practice in writing dates.

Listen carefully. Fill in every blank.

The _____ _____ the great ancient empires was the Roman Empire. This civilization of antiquity

began to crumble *in the 3rd Century A.D.* The _____

of the Roman Empire _____ _____ _____ the murder of Julius Caesar _____

_____ _____ . _____ his murder Caesar was the absolute dictator of the Roman

Empire _____ _____ _____ _____ _____ _____ . The _____ of the Roman

Empire actually _____ _____ as far as _____ or _____ _____ when the people of

Italy freed themselves from the Etruscans.

_____ the Roman Empire was the Greek civilization. The Greek states _____

to Alexander the Great ____ ____ ____ _____ ____ . In the century _____ _____

however, Greece enjoyed the Golden Age of Art and Culture _____ ____ ____ _____ _____ .

The Greek culture, in turn, _____ _____ _____ the island culture of

Crete — _____ _____ _____ . This was the so-called Minoan culture.

Looking _____ _____ Greece we recall the Persian Empire. The power of the Persian kings

was at its height in the century _____ _____ and _____ _____ . _____ _____ _____

the Persian Empire extended from India to Egypt.

turn the page

_____ _____ _____ we find the Egyptian and Babylonian Empires. During this period, the

oldest known code of law was developed by the Babylonian king, Hammurabi _____ _____ _____ or

___ _____ ____ . At _____ _____ _____ _____ the Egyptians built the

pyramids of Giza. The exact date of construction is unknown but it has been estimated ___ _____

___ _____ _____ and _ ____ __ _____ _____ .

The Egyptian and Babylonian cultures, of course, marked the end of prehistoric times and the beginning of written

history. Their period _____ _____ _____ ____ the year _____ _____ .

AURAL COMPREHENSION QUESTIONS

1. _____

2. _____

3. _____

4. _____

DISCUSSION TOPICS

1. Reverse chronological order.
2. Ancient empires.

VOCABULARY AND PRONUNCIATION

as early as	was preceded by	immediately preceding
as late as	before that	goes back even further
earlier still	date back	antiquity
back beyond	as far back as	ancient empires
prehistoric times	prior to	absolute dictator
written history	circa	began to crumble
in turn	pre-dating	power was at its height

(all names of empires and people in this lesson)

HOLIDAYS

"When is Thanksgiving Day? When is Memorial Day?"

The word "holiday" comes from the words "holy" and "day." Originally holidays were holy or religious days. Nowadays holidays include national, seasonal, and historical days of celebration. Here are some U.S. holidays. The ones marked with stars are designated by the government as legal holidays. Banks are not open on legal holidays and mail is not delivered.

Listen carefully. Write the date. Do NOT abbreviate. Be sure to write the complete phrase.

1. *New Year's Day *January 1st* _____

2. *Lincoln's Birthday _____

3. Valentine's Day _____

4. *Washington's Birthday (traditional date) _____

5. St. Patrick's Day _____

6. April Fool's Day _____

7. Easter _____

8. Mother's Day _____

9. *Memorial Day (traditional date) _____

10. Flag Day _____

11. Father's Day _____

12. *Independence Day _____

13. *Labor Day _____

14. *Columbus Day (traditional date) _____

15. Hallowe'en _____

16. Veterans Day (traditional date) _____

17. *Thanksgiving Day _____

18. *Christmas _____

AURAL COMPREHENSION QUESTIONS

1. _____

2. _____

3. _____

4. _____

DISCUSSION TOPICS

1. Holidays in your country.

2. Comparisons of holidays in different countries.

3. Categories or types of holidays, such as religious celebrations, national celebrations, seasonal celebrations, etc.

VOCABULARY AND PRONUNCIATION

holiday

national

seasonal

historical

celebration

legal holidays

(all names of holidays in this lesson)

EMERGING NATIONALISM

"When do you celebrate your Independence Day?"

Most of us can answer immediately. In the 200 years since the United States declared its independence from England, July 4, 1776, many countries have become independent nations. In the western hemisphere alone 26 countries have become independent. The colonial empires of Great Britain, Spain, France, Portugal, and the Netherlands disappeared as one nation after another became independent. This lesson is for writing months, days, and years.

Listen carefully. Write the independence date, as July 4, 1776. Be sure to use commas correctly.

Caribbean America

1. Barbados _____

2. Cuba _____

3. Dominican Republic _____

4. Haiti _____

5. Jamaica _____

6. Trinidad and Tobago _____

Central America

1. Costa Rica _____

2. El Salvador _____

3. Guatemala _____

4. Honduras _____

5. Nicaragua _____

6. Panama _____

South America

1. Argentina _____

2. Bolivia _____

3. Brazil _____

4. Chile _____

5. Colombia _____

6. Ecuador _____

7. Guyana _____

8. Paraguay _____

9. Peru _____

10. Uruguay _____

11. Venezuela _____

North America

1. Canada _____

2. Mexico _____

3. U.S.A. _____

AURAL COMPREHENSION QUESTIONS

1. _____

2. _____

3. _____

4. _____

DISCUSSION TOPIC

1. Emerging nationalism on the different continents.

VOCABULARY AND PRONUNCIATION

Independence Day

celebrate

declare independence

independent

nation

nationalism

emerge

emerging

western hemisphere

colonial empires

(all names of countries in this lesson)

CHEMICALS: NUMBERS, SYMBOLS, AND DATES

"When was radium discovered? What is the symbol for plutonium?"

Many chemical elements have been known to man since prehistoric times. Others are still being found today. Here are some of the most well-known elements. This lesson is for rapid review of numbers, letters, and dates.

Listen carefully. Write the atomic number, the letters used as the symbol for the element, and the date of discovery. Both the elements and the data will be given in random order. The elements are alphabetized for your convenience. Work as fast as possible.

Element	Atomic Number	Symbol	Date
1. Carbon			
2. Copper			
3. Gold			
4. Hydrogen			
5. Iron			
6. Lead			
7. Nickel			
8. Nitrogen			
9. Oxygen			
10. Radium			
11. Silicon			
12. Silver			
13. Sodium			
14. Tin			
15. Uranium			
16. Zinc			

AURAL COMPREHENSION QUESTIONS

1. _____

2. _____

3. _____

4. _____

_____

_____

DISCUSSION TOPIC

1. Values and uses of these chemicals.

VOCABULARY AND PRONUNCIATION

chemical

elements

prehistoric

atomic number

symbol

(all names of chemical elements in this lesson)

CHEMICAL DISCOVERIES

"What is the atomic number for calcium? When was zinc discovered?"

Prehistoric man knew lead and copper, silver and gold but never dreamed of the elements which were to be discovered in the 20th Century. This is another lesson for rapid review of numbers, letters, and dates.

Listen carefully. Write the atomic number, the letters used as the symbol for the element, and the date of discovery. Both the elements and the data will be given in random order. The elements are alphabetized for your convenience. Work as fast as possible.

Element	*Atomic Number*	*Symbol*	*Date*
1. Arsenic	_____	_____	_____
2. Bromine	_____	_____	_____
3. Calcium	_____	_____	_____
4. Chlorine	_____	_____	_____
5. Chromium	_____	_____	_____
6. Cobalt	_____	_____	_____
7. Fluorine	_____	_____	_____
8. Helium	_____	_____	_____
9. Iodine	_____	_____	_____
10. Magnesium	_____	_____	_____
11. Manganese	_____	_____	_____
12. Mercury	_____	_____	_____
13. Neon	_____	_____	_____
14. Phosphorus	_____	_____	_____
15. Platinum	_____	_____	_____
16. Potassium	_____	_____	_____
17. Sulfur	_____	_____	_____

SUGGESTION: Advanced Level students may wish to begin inserting lessons from Unit 8 at this point in order to begin more formal practice in note-taking.

AURAL COMPREHENSION QUESTIONS

1. _____

2. _____

3. _____

4. _____

_____

_____

DISCUSSION TOPIC

1. Values and uses of these chemicals.

VOCABULARY AND PRONUNCIATION

date of discovery

20th Century

(all names of chemical elements in this lesson)

EARLY EXPLORATIONS

Man's curiosity throughout time has sent him to explore the far-off places of the world. Sometimes he has explored for riches, sometimes for land, and sometimes for the pure adventure and joy of exploration.

Listen carefully. Write the dates. Write every word.

1. _____ Phoenician traders explored the west coast of Africa.

2. _____ Alexander the Great reached India.

3. _____ Greeks and Romans explored the Baltic.

4. _____ Ericsson, the Norseman, was probably the first European to reach North America.

5. _____ Marco Polo ventured to the Far East.

6. _____ the Great Age of Discovery began.

7. _____ all the known oceans were crossed.

8. _____ Columbus made his voyages to America.

9. _____ da Gama reached India.

10. _____ Balboa discovered the Pacific Ocean.

11. _____ Magellan's ship sailed around the world.

12. _____ Jacques Cartier discovered the St. Lawrence River and laid French claim to Canada.

13. _____ Francisco Coronado explored the southwestern U.S.

14. _____ John Cabot and his son Sebastian made Canadian discoveries for England.

15. _____ Vitus Bering discovered Alaska.

AURAL COMPREHENSION QUESTIONS

1. _____

2. _____

3. _____

4. _____

_____

_____

DISCUSSION TOPICS

1. Exploration.

2. Colonialism.

VOCABULARY AND PRONUNCIATION

early explorations	three centuries later
explore	The Great Age of Discovery
explorer	ventured to
around 200 B.C.	the known oceans
in the 1600's and 1700's	voyage
within 40 years	reached India
in 700 B.C.	discovery
in 1592	discovered
by 1692	sailed around the world
early in the 1500's	laid claim to
before the time of Christ	(all names of explorers and geographical locations in this lesson)

POPULATION MIGRATIONS

During the past 300 years great numbers of people have moved into new locations. Many Europeans migrated to the New World. Some of the people migrated to the Americas for religious reasons while others were motivated by political or economic reasons.

Listen carefully. Write the phrases as the teacher reads. Be *sure* to use the correct prepositions.

Europeans to U.S.A.

During _____ _____ _____ about _____ _____ _____ people emigrated from England to

the new North American colonies. Nearly three times that number followed _____ _____

_____ _____ from Ireland and Scotland. Germans, Italians, Scandinavians, Austrians, and

Hungarians followed _____ _____ _____ . _____ _____

_____ _____ a total of _____ _____ from a number of countries entered the

U.S. _____ _____ a single year record of _____ was

set. Immigrations were slow _____ _____ _____ _____ _____ with only _____

admitted. Another increase came _____ _____ _____ _____ with a total of _____ .

Europeans to Canada

Quebec was settled by the French _____ _____ _____ _____ . Settlement

was slow _____ _____ . It accelerated, however, _____ _____ _____ _____

when _____ _____ people entered from England. These were followed by _____

_____ in _____ _____ _____ _____ . _____ immigration

increased, with _____ _____ people _____ _____ _____ _____ .

Europeans to South and Central America

_____ _____ _____ _____ _____ nearly _____ _____ Europeans

migrated to Central and South America primarily from Spain, Portugal, and Italy. Immigration was slow _____

_____ _____ but reached its peak _____ _____ . _____ _____ _____

_____ about _____ _____ settled in Argentina. _____ _____ _____ _____ about

_____ _____ entered Brazil. _____ _____ _____ _____ saw internal

migrations throughout South and Central America.

AURAL COMPREHENSION QUESTIONS

1. _____

2. _____

3. _____

4. _____

_____

_____

DISCUSSION TOPICS

1. Migrations and reasons for migrations.

2. Contrast immigrant and emigrant.

VOCABULARY AND PRONUNCIATION

population migration	Europeans	North American colonies
emigrant	Canada	record was set
immigrant	South America	immigration increased
political reasons	Central America	immigration rate accelerated
religious reasons	Africa	primarily from Spain
economic reasons		internal migrations

thereafter	after 1650
to be followed by	until the turn of the century
during the 16th Century	from 1600 to 1630
in the next 20 years	from the end of the century
the period between 1840 and 1844	in the 17th Century
up to 1900	(all names in this lesson)

FORTUNE-TELLING CALENDARS

"Were you born under the sign of Aquarius? Were you born in the year of the Tiger?"
"Do you believe in the influence of the stars at the time of your birth?"

Find your birthdate in each of these two popular calendars.

Listen carefully. Write the dates.

THE ANCIENT GREEK ZODIAC CALENDAR: BASED ON A 12-MONTH CYCLE

1. *Capricorn*	4. *Aries*	7. *Cancer*	10. *Libra*
from _____	from _____	from _____	from _____
to _____	to _____	to _____	to _____
2. *Aquarius*	5. *Taurus*	8. *Leo*	11. *Scorpio*
from _____	from _____	from _____	from _____
to _____	to _____	to _____	to _____
3. *Pisces*	6. *Gemini*	9. *Virgo*	12. *Sagittarius*
from _____	from _____	from _____	from _____
to _____	to _____	to _____	to _____

THE ANCIENT CHINESE LUNAR CALENDAR: BASED ON A 12-YEAR CYCLE

1. The Year of the Rat	2. The Year of the Ox	3. The Year of the Tiger	4. The Year of the Rabbit
_____	_____	_____	_____
5. The Year of the Dragon	6. The Year of the Snake	7. The Year of the Horse	8. The Year of the Sheep
_____	_____	_____	_____
9. The Year of the Monkey	10. The Year of the Cock	11. The Year of the Dog	12. The Year of the Boar
_____	_____	_____	_____

PROBLEM

Notice that you can figure out the missing dates. In Part 1 let's look at Scorpio as an example. The *beginning* date for Scorpio is the day after the last day of Libra. The last day of Libra is October 22nd. Therefore, the first day of Scorpio is October 23rd. The *last* day of Scorpio is the day before the first day of Sagittarius. The first day of Sagittarius is November 22nd. Therefore, Scorpio ends on November 21st. Scorpio, then, is *from October 23rd to November 21st*. Now, figure out the other missing dates.

Part 2 is easy. Figure out the missing years based on a twelve-year cycle.

DISCUSSION TOPICS

1. Astrology.

2. Fortune-telling.

VOCABULARY AND PRONUNCIATION

influence   astrologer

zodiac   fortune-telling

astrology   fortune-teller

astrological   cycle

Lunar Animal Names

Rat	Rabbit	Horse	Cock
Ox	Dragon	Sheep	Dog
Tiger	Snake	Monkey	Boar

Zodiac Constellation Names

Sagittarius	= "The Archer"	Gemini	= "The Twins"
Scorpio	= "The Scorpion"	Taurus	= "The Bull"
Libra	= "The Scales"	Aries	= "The Ram"
Virgo	= "The Virgin"	Pisces	= "The Two Fish"
Leo	= "The Lion"	Aquarius	= "The Water-Bearer"
Cancer	= "The Crab"	Capricorn	= "The Sea-Goat"

HISTORY OF THE ENGLISH LANGUAGE

The English language can be traced back to prehistoric Indo-European through the West Germanic line. However, many other influences have shaped the development of Modern English. We will review some important dates in the history of the English language.

Listen carefully. Write all the information given. Write as fast as you can.

The first three are Latin influences:

1. _____

_____

2. _____

_____

3. _____

_____

The next significant dates were:

4. _____

_____

5. _____

_____

Influences from other languages:

6. _____

_____

Then,

7. _____

_____

8. _____

_____

9. _____

_____

And finally,

10. _____

_____

PROBLEM

From the data given, fill in the dates on the chart at the bottom of page 213.

DISCUSSION TOPICS

1. Development of the English language.

2. Vocabulary and pronunciation relationships to other languages.

VOCABULARY AND PRONUNCIATION

influences	Caesar conquered England
shaped	Rome colonized the island
Indo-European	Romans remained — Christian Era
West Germanic	Anglo-Saxon conquest of the island
Old English	West Germanic — the basic language of Britain
Middle English	England Christianized by missionaries sent by the Pope
Modern English	Vikings invaded — Old Norse language
Celtic	Norman Conquest — French linguistic influence
North Germanic	French influence continued for 3 centuries
Old Norse	classical learning revived — Latin influence again
Italic	
Latin	
French	

MEMORABLE EVENTS IN HISTORY

Important events occur in every century. Some influence the entire world. Some influence smaller areas. Let us look at some famous (and infamous) moments in history.

Listen carefully. Write the dates given. They are *not* all in correct chronological order.

1. _____ Indus Valley Civilization in India

2. _____ Pyramids begun in Egypt

3. _____ Romulus and Remus founded Rome (legend)

4. _____ Sinking of the Spanish Armada

5. _____ Mayan Calendar invented in Yucatan

6. _____ Parthenon completed in Athens

7. _____ Magna Carta signed

8. _____ Bubonic plague killed a quarter of Europe's population

9. _____ Constantinople captured by Ottoman Turks

10. _____ Mongol hordes conquered most of Central Asia and killed many

11. _____ Discovery of San Salvador (by Columbus)

12. _____ Anglo-Saxon migrations to Britain

13. _____ Slave trade begun to plantations of the Caribbean, Brazil, and southern U.S.

14. _____ First permanent settlement at Jamestown, Virginia, in the New World

PROBLEM

Look at the information you have written on page 215. Several events are not in correct chronological order. *Re-number* the events in correct chronological order.

DISCUSSION TOPICS

1. These historical events.

2. Chronological relationship of these events.

VOCABULARY AND PRONUNCIATION

well-developed	hordes
gigantic	massacred
legend	famous
unexpected	plantations
surprisingly	permanent
accurate	settlement
classic	established
dreadful	infamous
invading	(all names in this lesson)

FAMOUS MEN OF THE NINETEENTH AND TWENTIETH CENTURIES

History records the deeds of many famous men in each century. During the past two centuries many important changes have taken place. Let us look at some of the important men of this period.

Listen carefully. Write the dates given. Then match the names.

1. _____ _____   Bolívar
   (Russian statesman)

2. _____ _____   Churchill
   (Italian dictator)

3. _____ _____   Freud
   (British statesman)

4. _____ _____   Gandhi
   (Hindu leader)

5. _____ _____   Hitler
   (American president)

6. _____ _____   Kennedy
   (Prussian writer)

7. _____ _____   Lenin
   (American president)

8. _____ _____   Marx
   (South American liberator)

9. _____ _____   Mussolini
   (Austrian psychoanalyst)

10. _____ _____   Napoleon
    (Egyptian president)

11. _____ _____   Nassar
    (German dictator)

12. _____ _____   Nehru
    (Russian statesman)

13. _____ _____   Roosevelt
    (prime minister of India)

14. _____ _____   Stalin
    (French emperor)

PROBLEM

Look at page 217. Match each date with the correct name from the list at the right side of the page. Then choose three people who are related in some way in their activities. Put their names in chronological order. Write a short paragraph describing their relationship.

DISCUSSION TOPIC

1. Discuss the answers to this problem.

VOCABULARY AND PRONUNCIATION

life-span

statesman

dictator

leader

influential

assassinate

liberator

psychoanalyst

prime minister

emperor

(all names in this lesson)

CONFLICTS AND STRUGGLES

Numerous conflicts in the past two centuries have shaped our world today.

Listen carefully. Write the dates as the teacher dictates. Then write the event. Refer to the list at the bottom of the page.

1. _____ _____

2. _____ _____

3. _____ _____

4. _____ _____

5. _____ _____

6. _____ _____

7. _____ _____

8. _____ _____

9. _____ _____

10. _____ _____

11. _____ _____

12. _____ _____

13. _____ _____

14. _____ _____

15. _____ _____

16. _____ _____

(a) American Independence
(b) American Civil War
(c) Chinese Revolution/Sun Yat-Sen
(d) First Indian rebellion
(e) First World War (WWI)
(f) Greek War of Independence
(g) India becomes independent
(h) Korean War

(i) Mao Tse-tung/Communist control
(j) Mexican Revolution
(k) Napoleonic Wars
(l) Russian Revolution
(m) Second World War (WWII)
(n) Simon Bolívar ends Spanish power
(o) Six-Day Arab-Israeli War
(p) Vietnam War

PROBLEM

Look at page 219. Choose two related events and put them in chronological order. Write a short paragraph describing their relationship.

DISCUSSION TOPIC

1. Discuss the answers to the problem.

VOCABULARY AND PRONUNCIATION

war

conflict

struggle

revolution

rebellion

(all names in this lesson)

POPULATION EXPLOSION

Dates   Population Figures   Rates of Doubling

1. _____

2. _____

3. _____

4. _____

5. _____

6. _____

7. _____

8. _____

PROBLEM

In your opinion what will be the population situation during the *next* thirty years, 2000 to 2030?

DISCUSSION TOPICS

1. Population predictions.

2. Preventing over-population.

VOCABULARY AND PRONUNCIATION

overpopulation

rate of doubling

increased

decreased

PRACTICAL PROBLEMS WITH DATES (1)

Listen carefully. Write the information.

1. _____

_____

_____

_____

4. _____

_____

_____

_____

2. _____

_____

_____

_____

5. _____

_____

_____

_____

3. _____

_____

_____

6. _____

_____

_____

turn the page for # 7

7. _____

_____

_____

_____

9. _____

_____

_____

_____

8. _____

_____

_____

_____

10. _____

_____

_____

_____

TEST

Do the problems. Check your answers with your teacher.

PRACTICAL PROBLEMS WITH DATES (2)

Listen carefully. Write the information.

1. _____

   _____

   _____

   _____

2. _____

   _____

   _____

3. _____

   _____

   _____

4. _____

   _____

   _____

   _____

5. _____

   _____

   _____

6. _____

   _____

   _____

turn the page for # 7

7. _____   9. _____

_____   _____

_____   _____

_____   _____

8. _____   10. _____

_____   _____

_____   _____

_____   _____

TEST

Do the problems. Check your answers with your teacher.

VOCABULARY LIST
DATES/CHRONOLOGICAL RELATIONSHIPS

Write your personal list of new words. Please review this list and be sure you know each vocabulary item.

_____   _____

_____   _____

_____   _____

_____   _____

_____   _____

_____   _____

_____   _____

_____   _____

_____   _____

_____   _____

_____   _____

turn the page

VOCABULARY (continued)

_____   _____

_____   _____

_____   _____

_____   _____

_____   _____

_____   _____

_____   _____

_____   _____

_____   _____

_____   _____

_____   _____

_____   _____

Unit 6
Measurements and Amounts

Unit 6

Measurements and Amounts

Unit 6 is a short unit. It is designed to review several different kinds of measurements and to provide a little practice in context. In addition, important vocabulary is presented for study. Be sure to ask questions and discuss the unit with your teacher.

The first three *Review Lessons* review two standard systems of measurement and conversions between the two systems. Three additional *Review Lessons* emphasize phrases which tell relative number and amount, money exchange rates, and selected common instruments used in measuring a variety of quantities and qualities. Two *Context Lessons* are presented. One deals with temperatures in chemistry and weather. Another provides practice with measurements used in food packaging and pricing.

Two *Test Lessons* complete Unit 6. Both present practical problems in measurement.

THE METRIC SYSTEM OF MEASUREMENT
(CENTIMETER — GRAM — SECOND SYSTEM)

The meter is the base unit of the metric system of weights and measurements. The system is decimal throughout. The metric system was developed in France and adopted there in 1795-1799. Since that time many nations of the world have adopted the metric system. The meter was intended to be one ten-millionth (1/10,000,000) of the distance measured on the earth's surface from the equator to the pole. The legal length of the meter is the length of a platinum prototype bar kept near Paris since 1875 at the International Bureau of Weights and Measurements.

Listen carefully. This lesson will be given very rapidly.

Linear Measure

_____	millimeters (mm.)	= 1 centimeter (cm.)
_____	centimeters (cm.)	= 1 decimeter (dm.)
_____	decimeters (dm.)	= 1 meter (m.)
_____	meters (m.)	= 1 dekameter (Dm.)
_____	dekameters (Dm.)	= 1 kilometer (Km.)

Weight

_____	milligrams (mg.)	= 1 centigram (cg.)
_____	centigrams (cg.)	= 1 decigram (dg.)
_____	decigrams (dg.)	= 1 gram (g.)
_____	centigrams (cg.)	= 1 gram (g.)
_____	grams (g.)	= 1 dekagram (Dg.)
_____	grams (g.)	= 1 kilogram (kg.)
_____	kilograms (kg.)	= 1 ton (m.tn.)

Square Measure

_____	sq. mm.	= 1 sq. cm.
_____	sq. cm.	= 1 sq. dm.
_____	sq. cm.	= 1 sq. m.
_____	sq. m.	= 1 are
_____	ares	= 1 hectare
_____	hectares	= 1 sq. Km.

Cubic Measure

_____	cu. mm.	= 1 cu. cm. (1 c.c.)
_____	cu. cm.	= 1 cu. dm.
_____	cu. dm.	= 1 cu. m.

Liquid Measure

_____	milliliters (ml.)	= 1 centiliter (cl.)
_____	centiliters (cl.)	= 1 liter (l.)
_____	liters (l.)	= 1 kiloliter (kl.)

AURAL COMPREHENSION QUESTIONS

1. _____

2. _____

3. _____

4. _____

DISCUSSION TOPICS

1. Making conversions in this system.

2. Where is this system used?

3. Most commonly used measures.

VOCABULARY AND PRONUNCIATION

metric system

most commonly used measures: abbreviations:

centimeter		cm.
meter	linear measure	m.
kilometer		Km.
cubic meter	capacity measure	cu. m.
square meter		sq. m.
*are	surface measure	_____
*hectare		_____
liter	volume measure	l.
gram		g.
kilogram	weight	kg.
ton		m. tn.

prototype bar

platinum

*Pronounced / ar / and / hɛktar /.

THE FOOT-POUND-SECOND MEASUREMENT SYSTEM

The yard is basic to this system. The yard was supposed to have been established by King Henry I in England in the early 900's. It was said to be the distance from the tip of his nose to the end of his thumb when his arm was stretched to the fullest! Since 1893, however, the yard has been derived from the international prototype meter. The yard is 0.9144 of a meter and a pound is 0.4536 of a kilogram.

Listen carefully. Work as fast as possible.

Linear Measure

_____ inches (in.) = 1 foot (ft.)

_____ feet (ft.) = 1 yard (yd.)

_____ inches (in.) = 1 yard (yd.)

_____ feet (ft.) = 1 mile (mi.) (statute mile)

_____ feet (ft.) = 1 fathom (water depth)

_____ feet (ft.) = 1 nautical mile

Weight

_____ drams (dr.) = 1 ounce (oz.)

_____ ounces (oz.) = 1 pound (lb.)

_____ pounds (lb.) = 1 hundredweight (cwt.)

_____ pounds (lb.) = 1 ton

Dry Measure

_____ pints (pt.) = 1 quart

_____ pints (pt.) = 1 peck (pk.)

_____ pecks (pk.) = 1 bushel (bu.)
_____

Square Measure

_____ sq. in. = 1 sq. ft.

_____ sq. ft. = 1 sq. yd.

_____ sq. yd. = 1 (sq.) acre*

_____ (sq.) acres* = 1 sq. mi.

Cubic Measure

_____ cu. in. = 1 cu. ft.

_____ cu. ft. = 1 cu. yd.

Liquid Measure

_____ ounces (oz.) = 1 pint

_____ ounces (oz.) = 1 Imperial pint (Br.)

_____ cups = 1 pint

_____ pints (pt.) = 1 quart

_____ cups = 1 quart

_____ quarts (qt.) = 1 gallon

_____ gallon (gal.) = 1 Imperial gallon (Br.)

*The word _square_ does not need to be included with _acre_. Acre is a word which applies _only_ to square surface measurement.

AURAL COMPREHENSION QUESTIONS

1. _____

2. _____

3. _____

4. _____

DISCUSSION TOPICS

1. Making conversions in this system.

2. Where is this system used?

3. Most commonly used measures.

VOCABULARY AND PRONUNCIATION

most commonly used measures:

		abbreviations:
inch		in.
foot	linear measure	ft.
yard		yd.
mile		mi.
cubic foot	capacity measure	cu. ft.
cubic mile		cu. mi.
square foot		sq. ft.
acre	surface measure	_____
square mile		sq. mi.
quart	volume measure	qt.
gallon		gal.
ounce		oz.
pound	weight	lb.
ton		_____

Imperial gallon — Imperial pint

statute mile — nautical mile

fathom

CONVERSION TABLE

"What's the relationship between an inch and a centimeter?"
"What's the relationship between a pound and a kilogram?"
"What's the relationship between a mile and a kilometer?"

Some of the equivalences between the metric system and the system used in the United States will be reviewed in this lesson.

Listen carefully.

Common Measure	*Metric Equivalent*		*Approximation*	
1 inch	_____	cm.	_____	cm.
1 foot	_____	m.	_____	m.
1 yard	_____	m.	_____	m.
1 mile	_____	Km.	_____	Km.
1 acre	_____	hectare	_____	hectare
1 square mile	_____	sq. Km.	_____	sq. Km.
1 liquid quart	_____	l.	_____	l.
1 gallon (U.S.)	_____	l.	_____	l.
1 bushel	_____	l.	_____	l.
1 ounce	_____	g.	_____	g.
1 pound	_____	kg.	_____	kg.
1 ton	_____	m. tn.	_____	m. tn.

AURAL COMPREHENSION QUESTIONS

1. _____

2. _____

3. _____

4. _____

DISCUSSION TOPICS

1. Making conversions between the two systems.

2. Measurements used in your country.

VOCABULARY AND PRONUNCIATION

equivalent

convert

conversion

approximate

approximation

RELATIVE NUMBER: RELATIVE AMOUNT

"How much? How many?"

The word "many" expresses relative number and is used with count nouns. The word "much" expresses relative amount and is used with non-count nouns. Some phrases such as "a lot of" can be used with either count or non-count nouns. This lesson will review some common phrases of relative number and relative amount.

Listen carefully. Write the phrases.

	FRIENDS	BOTH	MONEY
1. Mary	__ _____ _____		__ _____ _____ __
2. Sam	_____		_____
3. George	__ _____ _____ __		__ _____ _____ __
4. Barbara		____ ____ ____	
5. Julia		_____ _____	
6. Harold	__ _____ _____ __		__ _____ ____ __
7. Helen	_____ _____		_____ _____
8. Frank		____ __ __ __	
9. Bill	_____		_____
10. Susan	_____ _____ _____		_____ ____ ____
11. Diana		_____ _____	
12. Betty		_____ _____	
13. David		_____	
14. Cynthia		___ ____ ____	
15. Jane		_____ ____ ___	

AURAL COMPREHENSION QUESTIONS

1. _____

2. _____

3. _____

4. _____

DISCUSSION TOPICS

1. Count and non-count nouns.

2. *General* value order of these phrases.

3. Contrast *few* and *a few; little* and *a little.*

4. Contrast *doesn't have any* and *doesn't have many.*

VOCABULARY AND PRONUNCIATION

With count nouns:	*With both:*	*With non-count nouns:*
a great many	a lot of	a great deal of
many	lots of	much
a large number of	doesn't have a lot of	a large amount of
an average number of	hardly any	a moderate amount of
a few	almost no	a little
few	no	little
doesn't have many	none	doesn't have much
	doesn't have any	

MONETARY SYSTEM AND EXCHANGE RATES

"How many dimes in a dollar? How many quarters? How much is the U.S. dollar worth?"

Coins of the United States are issued by the Bureau of the Mint. They are manufactured in Philadelphia, Denver, and San Francisco. Paper money is printed by the Bureau of Engraving in Washington, D.C. where stamps are also printed. The International Monetary Fund monitors exchange rates.

The rates included here are for a recent year but may have changed by now.

Listen carefully. Write the figures as dictated.

Part A: U.S. Monetary Values

	Dollars	Fifty-cent Pieces	Quarters	Dimes	Nickels	Pennies
1.	_____	_____	_____	_____	_____	_____
2.	_____	_____	_____	_____	_____	_____

(The following bills are also printed:

$5.00 $10.00 $20.00 $50.00 $100.00 $500.00 $1,000.00 $5,000.00 $10,000.00)

Part B: Selected Exchange Rates

	Country	Currency		U.S. Value Per Unit (rounded off to the nearest cent)
1.	Australia	1 Dollar	=	$ _____._____
2.	Brazil	1 Cruzeiro	=	_____._____
3.	Canada	1 Dollar	=	_____._____
4.	Costa Rica	1 Colon	=	_____._____
5.	Denmark	1 Krone	=	_____._____
6.	France	1 Franc	=	_____._____
7.	Germany (FR)	1 Deutsche Mark	=	_____._____
8.	Greece	1 Drachma	=	_____._____
9.	India	1 Rupee	=	_____._____
10.	Japan	1 Yen	=	_____._____
11.	Mexico	1 Peso	=	_____._____
12.	United Kingdom	1 Pound	=	_____._____

AURAL COMPREHENSION QUESTIONS

1. _____

2. _____

3. _____

4. _____

DISCUSSION TOPICS

1. Rates of exchange today.

2. Making change in U.S. money.

3. Changes in the British system.

VOCABULARY AND PRONUNCIATION

halves	dollars	pound*
quarters	monetary system	peso
dimes	exchange rates	yen
nickels	issue money	rupee
pennies	Bureau of the Mint	drachma
cents	Bureau of Engraving	Deutsche Mark
coins	International Monetary Fund	franc
paper money	monitor	krone
currency (money)		colon
		cruzeiro

_____

*Name each country.

SCIENTIFIC INSTRUMENTS FOR MEASUREMENT

"What is an altimeter? What does a compass measure? How are earthquakes measured?"

There are many many instruments which measure qualities and quantities. Michaelangelo, the famous painter and sculptor, was the inventor of many instruments.

Listen carefully. See if you can guess each answer before it is read. Then circle the correct letter.

1. an altimeter
   a. latitude
   b. altitude
   c. longitude

2. a barometer
   a. land elevation
   b. air pressure
   c. water depth

3. a compass
   a. direction
   b. temperature
   c. speed

4. a hygrometer
   a. weight
   b. temperature
   c. humidity

5. scales
   a. minutes
   b. weight
   c. depth

6. a seismograph
   a. hurricanes
   b. earthquakes
   c. floods

7. a sextant
   a. speed
   b. angular distance
   c. depth

8. a speedometer
   a. latitude
   b. speed
   c. angle

9. a tachometer
   a. mph
   b. rpm
   c. vip

10. a thermometer
    a. light
    b. weight
    c. temperature

11. an electrocardiograph
    a. heart beat
    b. brain waves
    c. lungs

12. an electroencephalograph
    a. hearing
    b. heart beat
    c. brain waves

13. an audiometer
    a. vision
    b. hearing
    c. breathing

14. a ruler
    a. weight
    b. length
    c. volume

15. a voltmeter
    a. electricity
    b. age
    c. depth

16. a yardstick
    a. age
    b. volume
    c. length

17. a protractor
    a. speed
    b. angles
    c. depth

18. an odometer
    a. distance
    b. altitude
    c. angle

19. a weather vane
    a. rainfall
    b. temperature
    c. wind direction

20. a tape measure
    a. distance
    b. weight
    c. heat

241

AURAL COMPREHENSION QUESTIONS

1. _____

2. _____

3. _____

4. _____

DISCUSSION TOPICS

1. Instruments in this exercise; other common instruments.

2. Quantities and qualities to be measured.

3. Categories such as weather, human body, etc.

VOCABULARY AND PRONUNCIATION

altimeter	electrocardiograph	weight	temperature
barometer	electroencephalograph	length	air pressure
compass	audiometer	width	atmospheric pressure
hygrometer	ruler	breadth	wind direction
scales	voltmeter	depth	rainfall
seismograph	yardstick	volume	humidity
sextant	protractor	distance	hurricanes
speedometer	weather vane	speed	earthquakes
tachometer		latitude	floods
thermometer		longitude	heart
		altitude	brain
		elevation	lungs
		direction	breathing
		angle	hearing
		light	vision
		heat	age
		electricity	
		revolutions per minute	

MEASUREMENTS IN CONTEXT: FAHRENHEIT AND CENTIGRADE SCALES

"What is the difference between 0 degrees Centigrade and 0 degrees Fahrenheit?"

Centigrade and Fahrenheit are both scales for measuring temperature. The Fahrenheit thermometer was developed in the early 1700's by a German physicist. On this scale the boiling point of water is 212 degrees and the freezing point is 32 degrees. The Centigrade scale was developed in 1742 by a Swedish astronomer. On this scale water boils at 100 degrees and freezes at 0 degrees. In scientific work the Centigrade scale usually is used.

Listen carefully. Use the symbol ° for degrees. Take notes of all the important facts.

Melting = _____

Boiling = _____

Part 1:   *Notes*   *Degrees Fahrenheit*

1. tungsten melts   _____   _____

2. iron boils   _____   _____

3. iron melts   _____   _____

4. gold melts   _____   _____

5. mercury boils   _____   _____

6. water boils   _____   _____

7. alcohol boils   _____   _____

8. paraffin melts   _____   _____

Part 2:

1. highest air temperature ever recorded   _____   _____

2. a very hot summer day   _____   _____

3. a pleasant summer day   _____   _____

4. a moderate winter day   _____   _____

5. water freezes   _____   _____

6. a very cold winter day   _____   _____

7. lowest air temperature ever recorded   _____   _____

8. absolute zero (all molecular motion ceases)   _____   _____

AURAL COMPREHENSION QUESTIONS

1. _____

2. _____

3. _____

4. _____

DISCUSSION TOPICS

1. When/where is the centigrade scale used?

2. When/where is the Fahrenheit scale used?

3. Uses of the different elements and compounds because of their particular properties.

4. Descriptions of weather; descriptions of the elements.

VOCABULARY AND PRONUNCIATION

elements	hard metallic element	medical uses
compounds	heavy magnetic element	industrial uses
properties	malleable metallic element	electrical uses
liquid state	heavy silver–white poisonous metallic element	waxy solid substance
gas	in the neighborhood of*	hydrocarbons
vapor	chemical compound	candles
melting point	two parts hydrogen	sealing wax
boiling point	one part oxygen	water-proofing
	volatile liquid	

―――――

*Informal – means "close to" or "approximately."

MEASUREMENTS IN CONTEXT:
FOOD PURCHASES — QUANTITY, MEASURE, AND PRICE

Food prices are very high in many countries. Meat, dairy products, and fresh fruits and vegetables are often some of the most expensive items.

Listen carefully. Write the quantity, unit, and price.

Quantity	*Unit*	*Item*	*Price Per Unit*
_____	_____	CANNED VEGETABLES	$ _____ . _____
_____	_____	EGGS	$ _____ . _____
_____	_____	LETTUCE	$ _____ . _____
_____	_____	BUTTER	$ _____ . _____
_____	_____	MILK	$ _____ . _____
_____	_____	ORANGE JUICE	$ _____ . _____
_____	_____	GROUND MEAT	$ _____ . _____
_____	_____	BEEF STEAK	$ _____ . _____
_____	_____	TOMATOES	$ _____ . _____
_____	_____	POTATOES	$ _____ . _____
_____	_____	BREAD	$ _____ . _____
_____	_____	SOUP	$ _____ . _____
_____	_____	SALT	$ _____ . _____
_____	_____	COFFEE	$ _____ . _____
_____	_____	SUGAR	$ _____ . _____
_____	_____	CRACKERS	$ _____ . _____
_____	_____	PRESERVES	$ _____ . _____
_____	_____	FLOUR	$ _____ . _____
_____	_____	PORK CHOPS	$ _____ . _____
_____	_____	CHICKEN	$ _____ . _____

AURAL COMPREHENSION QUESTIONS

1. _____

2. _____

3. _____

4. _____

DISCUSSION TOPICS

1. Answers to the questions.

2. Food prices today.

3. Classifications into food groups.

4. Contrast methods of food processing and packaging (i.e., raw, canned, frozen, smoked, cured) and related descriptive vocabulary.

VOCABULARY AND PRONUNCIATION

meats   a dozen eggs

dairy products   a pound of potatoes

canned food   a head of lettuce

produce   a 2-quart carton of milk

bakery goods   a sack of potatoes

staples   a loaf of bread

ten cents a can   a jar of preserves

ten cents a pound

MEASUREMENT PROBLEMS (1)

Listen carefully. Write the information.

1. _____   4. _____

_____   _____

_____   _____

_____   _____

2. _____   5. _____

_____   _____

_____   _____

_____   _____

3. _____   6. _____

_____   _____

_____   _____

turn the page for # 7

7. _____   9. _____

   _____   _____

   _____   _____

   _____   _____

8. _____   10. _____

   _____   _____

   _____   _____

   _____   _____

TEST

Finish the problems. Check your answers with your teacher.

MEASUREMENT PROBLEMS (2)

Listen carefully. Write the information.

1. _____

  _____

  _____

  _____

2. _____

  _____

  _____

3. _____

  _____

  _____

4. _____

  _____

  _____

  _____

5. _____

  _____

  _____

6. _____

  _____

  _____

turn the page for # 7

7. _____

_____

_____

_____

9. _____

_____

_____

_____

8. _____

_____

_____

_____

10. _____

_____

_____

_____

TEST

Finish the problems. Check your answers with your teacher.

VOCABULARY LIST — MEASUREMENTS

Write your personal list of new words. Please review this list and be sure you know each vocabulary item.

_____   _____

_____   _____

_____   _____

_____   _____

_____   _____

_____   _____

_____   _____

_____   _____

_____   _____

_____   _____

_____   _____

turn the page

VOCABULARY (continued)

_____   _____

_____   _____

_____   _____

_____   _____

_____   _____

_____   _____

_____   _____

_____   _____

_____   _____

_____   _____

_____   _____

_____   _____

_____   _____

Unit 7
Proportion, Comparison, and Contrast

Unit 7

Proportion, Comparison, and Contrast

Whereas Unit 6 emphasized simple measurements, Unit 7 deals with proportionate measurement and ways to compare and contrast data. The unit is designed to review and to practice simple statistical treatment. In addition, important vocabulary is presented for study. Ask questions and discuss.

The three *Review Lessons* include fractions, decimals, percentages, measurements of central tendency, proportion, ratio and correlation. Three *Context Lessons* present practice with American Council on Education survey figures, Department of Commerce statistics, and United Nations cost of living data.

Two *Problem Lessons* deal with United Nations population density information and foreign student enrollment in the United States. Last, two *Test Lessons* present practical problems.

FRACTIONS, DECIMALS, AND PERCENTAGES

Review these definitions:

1. A *fraction* is a quantity less than a whole number – expressed

with a numerator $\longrightarrow$ $\dfrac{2}{3}$ $\qquad$ $\dfrac{13}{14}$
and a denominator $\longrightarrow$

2. A *decimal fraction* is a fraction with an unwritten denominator of ten or some power of ten indicated by a point (decimal point) before the numerator as 0.5 or 0.05. The value of the denominator is determined by its place distance from the decimal point. (See page 256.)

3. *Percent* is an easy way to represent numbers named by fractions with the denominator of 100.

Thus, we have 3 forms: $\qquad$ $\dfrac{3}{4}$ $=$ 0.75 $=$ 75%

Listen carefully. Write the three forms.

	Figures	*Fraction*	*Decimal*	*Percent*
1.	_____	_____	_____	_____
2.	_____	_____	_____	_____
3.	_____	_____	_____	_____
4.	_____	_____	_____	_____
5.	_____	_____	_____	_____
6.	_____	_____	_____	_____
7.	_____	_____	_____	_____
8.	_____	_____	_____	_____

Look at the fractions. Reduce each to its simplest form.

AURAL COMPREHENSION QUESTIONS

1. _____

2. _____

3. _____

4. _____

DISCUSSION TOPICS

1. Reading decimals, fractions, and percentages.

2. Answers to the questions.

3. Contrast hundre*ds* and hundre*dths* and similar pairs.

VOCABULARY AND PRONUNCIATION

decimal fraction

decimal point

decimal place

round off

power of ten*

_____

fraction

whole number

reduce

fractional

numerator

denominator

integer*

percent

quantity

amount

_____

3.5	= three and five ten*ths*
3.05	= three and five hundre*dths*
3.005	= three and five thousan*dths*
3.0005	= three and five ten thousan*dths*
3.00005	= three and five hundred thousan*dths*
3.000005	= three and five million*ths*

_____

*Power of ten = multiplied ten times.
  Integer = whole number.

MEASUREMENTS OF CENTRAL TENDENCY

Measures of central tendency are used to show typical performance. They allow comparison and contrast of individuals or groups. Review these definitions:

1. The *mean* (i.e., the average) is the sum of all items divided by their number.

2. The *median* is the middlemost score. If items are arranged in rank order, one half of them will fall on each side of the median. (The median of 8, 11, *13*, 17, and 18 is 13; the median of 47, 52, *59*, 60, and 65 is 59.)

3. The *mode* is the item of greatest frequency in a series. (The mode is 70 here: 75 - 73 - *70 - 70 - 70* - 69 - 68.)

4. The *range* is the amount of spread in a distribution and is found by subtracting the smallest from the largest.

5. The *distribution* is the way items are grouped around the median and toward the extremes.

Listen carefully.

Group 1 – MEAN	Group 2 – MEDIAN	Group 3 – MODE
1. _____	1. _____	1. _____
2. _____	2. _____	2. _____
3. _____	3. _____	3. _____
4. _____	4. _____	4. _____
5. _____	5. _____	5. _____
6. _____	6. _____	6. _____
7. _____	7. _____	7. _____
8. _____	8. _____	8. _____
9. _____	9. _____	9. _____
10. _____		10. _____

AURAL COMPREHENSION QUESTIONS

1. _____

2. _____

3. _____

4. _____

DISCUSSION TOPICS

1. Practice with mean — median — and mode.

2. The answers to the questions.

VOCABULARY AND PRONUNCIATION

average

mean

median

mode

tendency

central tendency

range

extremes of a series

middlemost

rank order

typical

performance

frequency

distribution

PROPORTION, RATIO, AND CORRELATION

Review these definitions:

1. A *proportion* is a *part* of something in its relationship to the *whole* thing. Stating proportions allows us to compare parts of a whole.

   Example: The proportion of the votes was as follows: Forty percent voted *for* the amendment. Thirty-five percent voted *against* the amendment. Twenty-five percent remained *neutral.* Or, the proportion was forty *to* thirty-five *to* twenty-five.

2. *Ratio* is a special way of stating proportion. It is another way to state the relationship in number or percentage between two or more things.

   Example: In the class there is *a ratio of* three boys to two girls. That is, for every three boys there are two girls in the class. In other words, the *ratio is three to two* in favor of boys.

3. *Correlation* shows the close mutual relationship between two things. Often the relationship is a causal relationship. Sometimes it is complementary. (See definitions on page 260.)

   Example: In an industrial society there is a *high correlation* (i.e., relationship) between amount of industrialization and amount of air pollution.

Listen carefully. Write the percentage figures for each country, in each field.

	Agriculture	*Industry and Manufacturing*	*Commerce, Administration and Professions*
Egypt	_____	_____	_____
France	_____	_____	_____
United Kingdom	_____	_____	_____

AURAL COMPREHENSION QUESTIONS

1. _____

2. _____

3. _____

4. _____

DISCUSSION TOPICS

1. Practice with ratio, proportion, and correlation phrases.

2. The answers to the questions.

VOCABULARY AND PRONUNCIATION

proportion

ratio

correlation

for the amendment

against the amendment

neutral

mutual relationship*

causal relationship*

complementary relationship*

Mutual — two things having the same relationship toward each other.
  Causal — anything producing an effect or result.
  Complementary — something that completes or perfects another thing.

COLLEGE FRESHMEN: STATISTICAL INFORMATION

"How many students begin college as freshmen each year?"
"How is the average college education financed?"

Here are a few items from an American Council on Education survey.

Listen carefully. Fill in the blanks.

1. _____ _____ _____ students entered college last fall — _____

    _____ of last year's high school graduates.

2. They enrolled in _____ two-year, four-year, public, private, church-related and specialized colleges and universities.

3. In high school _____ _____ were A minus or better students.

4. But _____ _____ _____ _____ averaged C plus or lower.

5. _____ _____ had acceptances from _____ _____ _____ college.

6. _____ _____ reported their parent incomes as _____ _____ .

7. _____ _____ were _____ _____ .

8. Incomes of _____ _____ _____ were reported by _____ _____ .

9. Here is where most got financial support:*   personal savings or job _____

    family aid _____

    repayable loan _____

    scholarship, grant, gift _____

10. _____ _____ expected to participate in campus demonstrations.

11. But _____ _____ of them — _____ _____ _____ than last year — thought officials too lax with protesters.

12. _____ _____ _____ _____ said students should participate in curriculum planning.

_____

*Overlap in financial support results in a total of more than 100%.

AURAL COMPREHENSION QUESTIONS

1. _____

2. _____

3. _____

4. _____

DISCUSSION TOPICS

1. Answers to the questions.

2. Surveys, questionnaires, opinion polls, etc.

VOCABULARY AND PRONUNCIATION

almost a million	nearly half	about 10%
over half	below a hundred	some 5%
one out of ten	50 or more	a higher percentage
public colleges	A minus	personal savings
private colleges	C plus	participate
church-related colleges	acceptances	campus demonstrations
two-year colleges	income	lax
four-year colleges	financial support	protesters
specialized colleges		curriculum planning

GROSS NATIONAL PRODUCT AND CONSUMER PRICE INDEX

"What economic statistics give us meaningful information about a country?"
"What do the statistics mean?"

Each year the U.S. Department of Commerce prepares economic information about the preceding year. For practice in listening to and understanding some of the terminology we will use the statistics for a recent year.

Listen carefully. Fill in the blanks. Write down the word or the numbers as the teacher dictates.

1. The value of the goods and services produced — that is, the gross national product, or GNP — amounted to an

   annual _____ _____ _____ _____ in mid-1968, _____ _____ 1965.

2. The _____ _____ economic growth for 1960-1967 _____ _____ .

3. Personal income _____ _____ for the U.S. as a whole _____ ____ _____

   in 1967 compared with _____ in 1960, a _____ rise.

4. _____ of the fifty states were _____ the 1967 U.S. level; _____

   of the fifty states were _____ .

5. Connecticut _____ with _____ _____ _____ and Mississippi was

   _____ with _____ .

6. During the 1960 to mid-1968 period, wholesale prices rose _____ _____ _____

   and consumer prices rose _____ .

7. The _____ _____ in consumer prices, _____ , was in cost for medical

   care, followed by _____ for public transportation, _____ for shelter costs to home-

   owners, and _____ for food.

8. The _____ in consumer prices from 1960 to January — August 1968, meant that the

   purchasing power of the consumer dollar _____ by _____ _____ _____ _____ .

AURAL COMPREHENSION QUESTIONS

1. _____

2. _____

3. _____

4. _____

DISCUSSION TOPICS

1. Answers to the questions.

2. Wholesale versus consumer prices.

3. How meaningful is a per capita figure?

VOCABULARY AND PRONUNCIATION

value	above the level	purchasing power
annual rate	prices rose	consumer dollar
rate of growth	sharp rise	economic growth
averaged	decreased	personal income
per capita	declined	goods and services
amounted to	fell	gross national product
compared with	consumer prices	GNP
	wholesale prices	

COST OF LIVING COMPARISONS

"What is the cost of living in France? In Liberia?"

This comparison of the cost of living in selected countries of the world was prepared by the United Nations Statistical Bureau. It is based on the prices for goods, services, and housing for international officials stationed in each country — in its capital city. The relative costs are based on approximately 120 items.

The index figure of 100 was assigned to New York City. Here is an example to illustrate the cost comparison: if an item cost $1.00 in New York, the same item bought in London would cost $0.70 because the index shows 70 for London. On the other hand, the same item would cost $1.02 in Paris because the index shows the figure 102 for Paris.

Listen carefully. Write down the amount in dollars and cents, as $1.19 or $.45.

Group 1

The capitals of the following countries had relatively high costs of living:

Republic of Congo	_____	Mauritania _____
Chad	_____	Liberia _____
Ivory Coast	_____	Cameroon _____
Upper Volta	_____	Togo _____
Nigeria	_____	Saudi Arabia _____

Group 2

On the other hand the capitals of the following countries had relatively low costs of living:

Malawi	_____	Guyana _____
Ceylon	_____	Jamaica _____
Afghanistan	_____	Argentina _____
Uruguay	_____	Syria _____
United Kingdom	_____	Republic of China _____

AURAL COMPREHENSION QUESTIONS

1. _____

2. _____

3. _____

4. _____

DISCUSSION TOPICS

1. Answers to the questions.

2. Reasons for differences in cost of living.

VOCABULARY AND PRONUNCIATION

cost of living

comparison

relative costs

index figure

DENSITY OF POPULATION

"What is the population? What is the land area? How many people per square mile?"

Let us examine some population statistics.

Listen carefully.

Place	Population	Land Area*
1. _____	_____	3,800,000 sq. mi.
2. _____	_____	1,266,210 sq. mi.
3. _____	_____	8,649,500 sq. mi.
4. _____	_____	3,615,211 sq. mi.
5. _____	_____	575,450 sq. mi.
6. _____	_____	364,737 sq. mi.
7. _____	_____	142,700 sq. mi.
8. _____	_____	3,286,170 sq. mi.
9. _____	_____	373,250 sq. mi.
10. _____	_____	95,915 sq. mi.

_____

*In square miles

PROBLEM

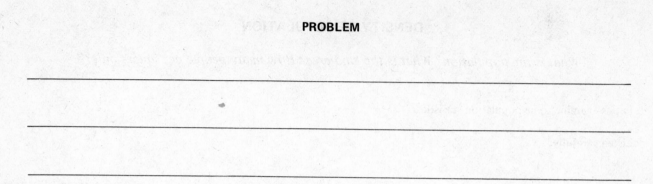

_____

_____

_____

DISCUSSION TOPICS

1. Answers to the above problem.

2. Population problems.

VOCABULARY AND PRONUNCIATION

density

low density

high density

densely populated

people per square mile

FOREIGN STUDENTS IN THE UNITED STATES

Each year many students from countries around the world come to study in the United States. Many of them enroll in intensive English courses before they begin academic study in their professional fields. Here are one-semester statistics from a leading university in the United States for the top fifteen countries.

Listen carefully. Write the country and the number of students.

_____   _____

_____   _____

_____   _____

_____   _____

_____   _____

_____   _____

_____   _____

_____   _____

_____   _____

_____   _____

PROBLEM

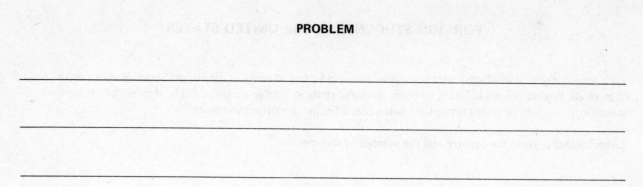

DISCUSSION TOPICS

1. Answers to the above problem.

2. Foreign student enrollments.

VOCABULARY AND PRONUNCIATION

enroll

intensive course

academic study

professional fields

one-semester

leading university

PROPORTION PROBLEMS (1)

Listen carefully. Write the information.

1. _____

_____

_____

_____

2. _____

_____

_____

_____

3. _____

_____

_____

_____

turn the page for # 4

4. _____

_____

_____

_____

5. _____

_____

_____

_____

6. _____

_____

_____

_____

TEST

Do the problems. Check your answers with your teacher.

PROPORTION PROBLEMS (2)

Listen carefully. Write the information.

1. _____

   _____

   _____

   _____

   _____

2. _____

   _____

   _____

   _____

3. _____

   _____

   _____

   _____

turn the page for # 4

4. _____

_____

_____

_____

_____

5. _____

_____

_____

_____

_____

6. _____

_____

_____

_____

_____

TEST

Do the problems. Check your answers with your teacher.

VOCABULARY LIST
PROPORTION, COMPARISON, AND CONTRAST

Write your personal list of new words. Please review this list and be sure you know each vocabulary item.

_____ _____

_____ _____

_____ _____

_____ _____

_____ _____

_____ _____

_____ _____

_____ _____

_____ _____

_____ _____

turn the page

VOCABULARY (continued)

_____   _____

_____   _____

_____   _____

_____   _____

_____   _____

_____   _____

_____   _____

_____   _____

_____   _____

_____   _____

_____   _____

_____   _____

_____   _____

Unit 8
Getting the Facts – Practice Readings

Unit 8

Getting the Facts – Practice Readings

In the preceding seven units you have practiced listening, remembering, and writing facts in each of these CONCEPT areas: numbers, letters, directions, times, dates, measurements, and proportions. In addition, the lessons have given you practice with facts involving people, places, things, actions, events, and descriptions in the CONTENT areas of: geography, history, science, mathematics, language, culture and customs, government, economics, and international affairs.

Unit Eight puts it all together. It combines all kinds of facts in a series of fifteen practice readings. It is your job to get the facts.

The directions are the same for each of these lessons. Study the vocabulary. Listen to the reading. Write notes of all the important facts. Listen to the questions. Write the answers.

When you have finished the lessons in Unit Eight you are ready for longer and more complex readings.

THE ENGLISH DICTIONARY

1. Vocabulary:

exhaustive   Webster's New World Dictionary

college edition   entry (in a dictionary)

prefix form

2. Notes:

_____

_____

_____

_____

_____

_____

_____

3. Answers to Questions:

_____

_____

_____

_____

_____

ENGLISH AND THE INDO-EUROPEAN FAMILY OF LANGUAGES

1. **Vocabulary:**

ancient	broad	descendant
scholar	scope	geographic location
linguists	descended from	present-day
Europe	things in nature	comparative language study
Indo-European	prehistoric	

2. **Notes:**

_____

_____

_____

_____

_____

_____

_____

_____

3. **Answers to Questions:**

_____

_____

_____

_____

_____

GOLD

1. **Vocabulary:**

fineness	dissolved	troy ounce
carat	estimated	bar
alloy	world standard	Ft. Knox, Kentucky
rushing	Gold Rush	

2. **Notes:**

_____

_____

_____

_____

_____

_____

_____

_____

3. **Answers to Questions:**

_____

_____

_____

_____

_____

_____

MAN AND THE MOON

1. Vocabulary:

Jules Verne	spaceship	stepped out
amazing	similarities	predicted
accuracy	initial speed	Apollo 11

2. Notes:

_____

_____

_____

_____

_____

_____

_____

3. Answers to Questions:

_____

_____

_____

_____

_____

_____

BASEBALL — A GOOD BATTING AVERAGE

1. **Vocabulary:**

professional teams	bat
baseball league	batter
Major League teams	batting average
headquarters	bases
runs	stick
	percentage of success

2. **Notes:**

_____

_____

_____

_____

_____

_____

_____

3. **Answers to Questions:**

_____

_____

_____

_____

_____

_____

STRUCTURE OF GOVERNMENT

1. Vocabulary:

separation of power	upper house	judicial branch
theory	lower house	Supreme Court
branch	regardless	appointed
constitution	executive branch	approval
legislative branch	cabinet	a two-year term

2. Notes:

_____

_____

_____

_____

_____

_____

_____

3. Answers to Questions:

_____

_____

_____

_____

_____

_____

THE INTERNATIONAL ICE PATROL

1. Vocabulary:

smashed into	shipping lanes	collision
iceberg	aircraft	Newfoundland
drowned	glacier	ocean currents
tragedy	drifting past	Titanic

2. Notes:

_____

_____

_____

_____

_____

_____

_____

_____

3. Answers to Questions:

_____

_____

_____

_____

_____

WORLD ENVIRONMENTAL CONFERENCE

1. **Vocabulary:**

environment	waste products	soil
uses up	garbage	erosion
natural resources	pollution	carbon dioxide
discard	cut down	capture
food crops	killed off	

2. **Notes:**

_____

_____

_____

_____

_____

_____

_____

3. **Answers to Questions:**

_____

_____

_____

_____

_____

AUDIO

1. **Vocabulary:**

auditory sense	pitch	loudness level
frequency	cycles per second	just above
tone	decibels	thunder
whisper		

2. **Notes:**

_____

_____

_____

_____

_____

_____

_____

3. **Answers to Questions:**

_____

_____

_____

_____

_____

_____

VIDEO

1. **Vocabulary:**

sight	phenomena	spectrum
visual sense	millimicrons	light-wave
sensitive	range	detect
shades of color		

2. **Notes:**

_____

_____

_____

_____

_____

_____

_____

3. **Answers to Questions:**

_____

_____

_____

_____

_____

_____

SUPERSONIC SPEED AND TRANSPORTATION OF THE FUTURE

1. Vocabulary:

super	physicist	Concorde
Ernst Mach	aerodynamics	altitude
Mach I	supersonic	

2. Notes:

_____

_____

_____

_____

_____

_____

_____

3. Answers to Questions:

_____

_____

_____

_____

_____

_____

WORLD DEMOGRAPHY

1. **Vocabulary:**

demographic experts

dawn of civilization

acceleration

geometric progression

disease

sequence

expanding

medical advances

density

epidemics

2. **Notes:**

_____

_____

_____

_____

_____

_____

_____

_____

3. **Answers to Questions:**

_____

_____

_____

_____

_____

_____

_____

RICHES FROM THE SEA

1. Vocabulary:

riches	expanded
wealth	buried beneath
fuel	vast
oceanographers	supplies
harvesting	natural resources

2. Notes:

_____

_____

_____

_____

_____

_____

_____

3. Answers to Questions:

_____

_____

_____

_____

_____

_____

STATUS OF THE NATIONS OF THE WORLD

1. Vocabulary:

status	a big jump	politico-geographical
quasi-independent	breakup	the term
jurisdiction	colonial empires	corresponds
aspects	the other extreme	the Vatican
emerging nationalism		

2. Notes:

_____

_____

_____

_____

_____

_____

_____

3. Answers to Questions:

_____

_____

_____

_____

_____

U.S. GEOGRAPHY

1. **Vocabulary:**

original states	Texas	altitude
the Union	Rhode Island	Mount McKinley
recent additions	border to border	Death Valley
Hawaii	California	Nevada
Alaska		

2. **Notes:**

_____

_____

_____

_____

_____

_____

_____

3. **Answers to Questions:**

_____

_____

_____

_____

_____

LIST OF WORKBOOK LESSON TITLES*

---

*R = Review Lesson
C = Context Lesson
P = Problem Lesson
T = Test Lesson

UNIT 7 – PROPORTION, COMPARISON, AND CONTRAST

UNIT 8 – GETTING THE FACTS – PRACTICE READINGS